2024

AGILITY UNBOUND

ASISH DASH

Agility Unbound:

Harnessing the Power of Adaptive Organizations

Table of Contents

Page intentionally left blank

Page intentionally left blank

Dedication

To my beloved daughter,

As I hold you in my arms and gaze into your innocent eyes, I am overwhelmed with a love so profound that it defies description. Your arrival has brought immeasurable joy and purpose to my life, and I am forever grateful for the privilege of being your father.

This book is a labor of love, a culmination of years of research, hard work, and passion. But it pales in comparison to the love I have for you, my little one. You have become my greatest inspiration, my driving force, and my reason for being.

As you grow and embark on your own journey, I hope that this book will be a tangible expression of my love for you, a reminder that no matter where life takes you, you will always have a father who believes in you, who supports you, and who loves you unconditionally.

With all my love,

Page intentionally left blank

Preface

In a world where change is the only constant, where disruption is the norm, and where uncertainty reigns supreme, how do organizations not only survive but thrive?

The answer lies in one word: agility.

But what does it really mean to be agile, and how can we harness its power to create truly adaptive organizations?

This book, *"Agility Unbound: Harnessing the Power of Adaptive Organizations,"* is the culmination of my own journey to answer these questions.

As an entrepreneur, author, and lifelong learner, I have witnessed firsthand the transformative power of agility in driving innovation, growth, and success. Through extensive research, interviews with industry leaders, and my own personal experiences, I have come to believe that agility is not just a buzzword or a passing trend, but a fundamental shift in the way we approach work, leadership, and organizational design.

In the pages that follow, I will explore the key principles and practices of agility, drawing on examples and insights from a wide range of industries and contexts. From the importance of adaptability and resilience to the role of collaboration and experimentation, I will provide a roadmap for organizations looking to break free from the shackles of traditional hierarchies and bureaucracies and embrace a more dynamic, responsive, and adaptive approach to work.

But this book is not just about theory or abstract concepts. It is also a deeply personal reflection on my own journey. It is my hope that by sharing my own experiences and lessons learned, I can inspire and empower others to unleash the power of agility in their own organizations and lives.

Whether you are an executive looking to lead your organization through transformation, a team member seeking to drive innovation and growth, or simply someone who is curious about the future of work and leadership, this book has something to offer.

So join me on this journey of discovery and transformation, and let us unlock the power of agility together.

Asish Dash

April 2024

Page intentionally left blank

Introduction: The Importance of Agility in Modern Business

In today's fast-paced, ever-changing business landscape, the ability to adapt quickly and effectively has become a critical factor for success. Gone are the days when companies could rely on static five-year plans and rigid hierarchies to navigate the challenges of the marketplace.

The rise of disruptive technologies, shifting consumer preferences, and global economic uncertainties have made one thing clear: *Agility is no longer a luxury, but a necessity.*

But what exactly do we mean by agility in a business context?

At its core, agility is about being able to respond rapidly and flexibly to changes in the environment. It's about embracing a mindset of continuous improvement, experimentation, and learning.

Agile organizations are those that can quickly pivot their strategies, reallocate resources, and adapt their processes to seize new opportunities or mitigate emerging threats. The benefits of agility are numerous and far-reaching. Research by McKinsey & Company found that agile organizations outperform their peers in both financial performance and customer satisfaction. In a study of more than 2,500 companies across industries, those that embraced agile practices saw 30% higher profits and 50% higher revenue growth compared to non-agile firms.

One powerful example of agility in action is the story of Nokia.

Once the world's dominant mobile phone manufacturer, Nokia found itself struggling to keep up with the rapid shift to smartphones in the late 2000s. While competitors like Apple and Samsung quickly adapted to the changing market, Nokia remained stuck in its ways, relying on its legacy Symbian operating system and failing to innovate. By the time the company finally embraced agility and launched its Lumia line of Windows phones in 2011, it was too late. Nokia's market share plummeted from 40% in 2007 to less than 5% by 2013, and the company was eventually acquired by Microsoft.

On the flip side, consider the success of Spotify, the world's largest music streaming service.

From its inception, Spotify has embraced agility as a core part of its culture and operations. The company is organized into small, autonomous teams called "squads" that are responsible for specific features or areas of the product. These squads operate with a high degree of autonomy, allowing them to experiment, iterate, and deliver value to customers quickly. Spotify also employs a unique "guild" system, where employees with similar skills and interests can collaborate across squads to share knowledge and best practices. This agile approach has enabled Spotify to continuously innovate and improve its product, even as it has scaled to over 350 million users globally. The company's ability to adapt to changing consumer preferences, such as the rise of podcasts and personalized playlists, has kept it ahead of competitors like Apple Music and Amazon Music.

But agility isn't just about responding to external changes; it's also **about proactively driving change from within.**

Agile organizations foster a culture of experimentation and calculated risk-taking, encouraging employees to challenge the status quo and propose new ideas. They embrace failure as a learning opportunity rather than something to be avoided at all costs.

Take Amazon, for example.

The e-commerce giant is known for its "Day 1" philosophy, which emphasizes a startup mentality of constant innovation and customer obsession. Employees are encouraged to think like owners and propose bold ideas, even if they may fail. This culture of experimentation has led to groundbreaking innovations like Amazon Prime, Amazon Web Services, and Alexa, which have transformed entire industries.

Of course, embracing agility is easier said than done.

It requires a fundamental shift in mindset and a willingness to let go of long-held assumptions and practices. Many organizations struggle with the transition from traditional, hierarchical structures to more fluid, networked ones. There can be resistance from employees who are comfortable with the status quo or fear losing control.

To overcome these challenges, leaders must actively champion agility and model the behaviours they wish to see in their teams.

They must create an environment of psychological safety, where employees feel empowered to take risks and voice dissenting opinions.

They must also invest in the tools, processes, and training necessary to support agile ways of working.

One framework that can help organizations become more agile is the "Agile Fluency Model," developed by James Shore and Diana Larsen. The model outlines four stages of agile fluency, from focusing on value delivery to optimizing for systems-level performance. By assessing their current stage and identifying the practices and behaviours needed to progress to the next level, organizations can create a roadmap for their agile transformation.

Another useful tool is the "Agile Maturity Matrix," which helps organizations evaluate their agility across various dimensions such as culture, leadership, and processes. By regularly assessing their maturity level and identifying areas for improvement, organizations can continuously evolve and adapt to changing circumstances.

Ultimately, the importance of agility in modern business cannot be overstated.

In a world where change is the only constant, the ability to pivot quickly and effectively is a key differentiator between success and failure. By embracing agility as a core part of their culture and operations, organizations can unlock new levels of innovation, resilience, and growth.

But the benefits of agility extend beyond just financial performance.

Agile organizations are also better equipped to attract and retain top talent, as employees increasingly seek out workplaces that offer autonomy, purpose, and opportunities for growth. They are more responsive to customer needs and feedback, leading to higher levels of satisfaction and loyalty. And they are better positioned to navigate the complex social and environmental challenges facing businesses today, from climate change to social inequality.

As we'll explore throughout this book, becoming an agile organization is a journey, not a destination. It requires ongoing commitment, experimentation, and learning. But for those willing to embrace the challenge, the rewards are immense.

By unlocking the power of agility, businesses can not only survive but thrive in an increasingly uncertain and rapidly changing world.

Exercise: Assess Your Organization's Agility

Take a few minutes to reflect on your own organization's level of agility.

Consider the following questions:

1. How quickly can your organization respond to changes in the market or customer needs?

2. Do employees feel empowered to experiment and propose new ideas, even if they may fail?

3. Are decisions made quickly and autonomously, or do they require multiple layers of approval?

4. Is your organization structured in a hierarchical or networked way?

5. Do you have processes in place to regularly assess and improve your agility?

Based on your answers, identify one or two areas where your organization could improve its agility.

What specific actions could you take to address these areas?

Share your reflections with a colleague or team member and discuss how you can work together to drive greater agility in your organization.

Key Benefits of Adopting an Agile Approach

In the previous section, we touched on some of the high-level benefits of agility, such as improved financial performance and customer satisfaction.

Now, let's dive deeper into the specific advantages that agile organizations enjoy over their more traditional counterparts.

1. Faster Time-to-Market

One of the most significant benefits of agility is the ability to bring new products and services to market faster. By breaking down large projects into smaller, iterative chunks, agile teams can deliver value to customers more frequently and with less risk. This approach allows organizations to test and validate ideas quickly, gather feedback, and make adjustments based on real-world data.

Consider the case of Zara, the global fashion retailer.

While most fashion brands take months to design, manufacture, and ship new collections, Zara has optimized its supply chain to be incredibly agile. The company can design, produce, and deliver new styles to stores in as little as two weeks, allowing it to quickly respond to changing fashion trends and customer preferences. This agility has helped Zara become one of the most valuable apparel brands in the world, with over 2,200 stores in 96 countries.

2. Enhanced Customer Centricity

Agile organizations are obsessed with delivering value to their customers.

By involving customers in the development process early and often, agile teams can ensure that they are building products and services that truly meet customer needs. This customer-centric approach leads to higher levels of satisfaction, loyalty, and advocacy.

One company that exemplifies this customer-centric mindset is Airbnb.

From its early days as a startup, Airbnb has relied on customer feedback to guide its product development and business strategy. The company regularly conducts user research, usability testing, and surveys to understand the needs and preferences of its hosts and guests. This deep understanding of its customers has helped Airbnb create a platform that delivers personalized, authentic travel experiences to millions of users worldwide.

3. Increased Employee Engagement and Productivity

Agile organizations empower their employees to take ownership of their work and make decisions autonomously. This level of trust and autonomy can lead to higher levels of engagement, motivation, and productivity. When employees feel that their contributions are valued and that they have the freedom to experiment and innovate, they are more likely to go above and beyond in their roles.

A great example of this is Google, which is known for its highly engaged and productive workforce.

Google encourages its employees to spend 20% of their time working on projects that interest them personally, even if they are not directly related to their job responsibilities. This "20% time" policy has led to the creation of some of Google's most successful products, such as Gmail and AdSense. By giving employees the autonomy to pursue their passions and take risks, Google has fostered a culture of innovation and creativity that is the envy of many organizations.

4. Improved Collaboration and Communication

Agile organizations prioritize collaboration and communication across teams and departments. By breaking down silos and encouraging cross-functional cooperation, agile teams can leverage diverse perspectives and skills to solve complex problems and deliver better results. Agile practices like daily stand-ups, retrospectives, and co-located teams help to foster a culture of transparency, trust, and continuous improvement.

One company that has mastered the art of collaboration is Pixar Studios.

Pixar's creative process is highly collaborative, with animators, writers, and technicians working closely together throughout the production of each film. The studio has developed a unique "Braintrust" process, where a group of experienced filmmakers provide candid feedback and suggestions on each project at regular intervals. This collaborative approach has helped Pixar create some of the most beloved and successful animated films of all time, from Toy Story to Inside Out.

5. Greater Resilience and Adaptability

In today's rapidly changing business environment, the ability to adapt and pivot quickly is essential for long-term success. Agile organizations are inherently more resilient and adaptable than their more rigid counterparts. By embracing change as a constant and building flexibility into their processes and structures, agile organizations can quickly respond to new challenges and opportunities as they arise.

A powerful example of this resilience in action is the story of Slack.

When the COVID-19 pandemic hit in early 2020, Slack saw a massive surge in demand as companies around the world shifted to remote work. The company's agile infrastructure and culture allowed it to quickly scale its operations and support the influx of new users, all while maintaining high levels of reliability and performance. Slack's ability to adapt to the new reality of work helped it become an essential tool for millions of remote workers and cemented its position as a leader in the collaboration software market.

6. Continuous Learning and Improvement

Finally, agile organizations are committed to continuous learning and improvement. By regularly reflecting on their successes and failures, and using data to guide their decision-making, agile teams can identify areas for optimization and experimentation. This mindset of continuous improvement helps organizations stay ahead of the curve and avoid the pitfalls of complacency and stagnation.

A great example of this learning mindset is Amazon's "Day 1" philosophy, which we mentioned earlier.

By treating every day as if it were the first day of a startup, Amazon encourages its employees to embrace a beginner's mindset and constantly look for ways to improve the customer experience. This focus on continuous learning has helped Amazon expand beyond its roots as an online bookstore to become a global leader in e-commerce, cloud computing, and artificial intelligence.

Exercise: Identify Agility Opportunities

Think about your own organization and how it could benefit from greater agility. Consider the following questions:

1. What are some areas where your organization could bring new products or services to market faster?

2. How could your organization involve customers more deeply in the development process to ensure better alignment with their needs?

3. What are some ways your organization could empower employees to take greater ownership of their work and make decisions autonomously?

4. How could your organization break down silos and encourage greater collaboration and communication across teams?

5. What are some examples of how your organization has adapted to change in the past, and how could it become even more resilient and adaptable in the future?

6. How could your organization foster a culture of continuous learning and improvement, and what metrics could you use to track progress over time?

Based on your reflections, identify one or two specific initiatives that your organization could undertake to become more agile.

What resources would be required, and what benefits could you expect to see as a result? Share your ideas with your team and leadership, and start a conversation about how to turn these opportunities into reality.

Overview of the Book's Structure and Objectives

Now that we've explored the importance of agility and the key benefits it offers, let's take a closer look at what you can expect from the rest of this book.

Our goal is to provide you with a comprehensive, practical guide to unlocking the power of agility in your organization, no matter your industry, size, or current level of agile maturity.

The book is divided into four main parts, each building on the concepts and strategies introduced in the previous sections.

Here's a brief overview of what we'll cover:

Part 1: Understanding Agility In the first part of the book, we'll lay the foundation for your agile transformation by exploring the core concepts and principles of agility. We'll start by defining what we mean by "business agility" and contrasting it with more traditional, hierarchical approaches to management.

Next, we'll dive into the mindset and culture shifts required to truly embrace agility, including the role of leadership in fostering an agile environment. Finally, we'll introduce some of the most popular agile frameworks and methodologies, such as Scrum, Kanban, and Lean, and help you determine which approach might be best suited for your organization.

Part 2: Implementing Agility Across Business Functions Once you have a solid understanding of the agile mindset and principles, we'll turn our attention to the practical application of agility across various business functions.

From strategy and planning to marketing, sales, operations, finance, and HR, we'll explore how agile practices can be adapted and integrated into every aspect of your organization. Through real-world examples, case studies, and practical exercises, you'll gain a deeper understanding of how to implement agility in your specific context and overcome common challenges along the way.

Part 3: Agile Transformation and Scaling In the third part of the book, we'll tackle the complex topic of organizational transformation and scaling agility beyond individual teams. We'll start by assessing your organization's readiness for change and developing a customized roadmap for your agile journey.

Next, we'll introduce several frameworks for scaling agility, such as SAFe (Scaled Agile Framework) and LeSS (Large-Scale Scrum), and explore the trade-offs and considerations of each approach. Finally, we'll discuss the importance of measuring the impact of your agile initiatives and continuously improving based on data and feedback.

Part 4: Agility in Action The final part of the book is all about bringing agility to life through real-world examples and forward-looking insights. We'll showcase a diverse range of case studies from organizations across industries and regions that have successfully embraced agility and reaped the benefits.

From startups to Fortune 500 companies, you'll learn valuable lessons and best practices that you can apply to your own agile journey. We'll also explore the future of work and how agility can help organizations adapt to emerging trends and challenges, such as remote and hybrid work, digital transformation, and the increasing importance of sustainability and social responsibility.

Throughout the book, our objective is to provide you with a balance of theoretical knowledge and practical tools to help you navigate the complex landscape of agility.

We'll introduce several original frameworks and models, such as the "Agile Fluency Model" and the "Agile Maturity Matrix," to help you assess your current state and identify areas for improvement. We'll also include interactive exercises, reflection questions, and action plans to help you internalize the concepts and apply them to your specific context.

Our ultimate goal is to empower you to become a champion of agility within your organization, armed with the knowledge, skills, and confidence to drive meaningful change. Whether you're a seasoned agile practitioner or just starting your journey, this book will provide you with a comprehensive roadmap for unlocking the full potential of agility and thriving in an increasingly uncertain and rapidly changing world.

So, let's dive in and start exploring the exciting world of agility together!

In the next chapter, we'll begin by defining what we mean by "business agility" and why it matters more than ever in today's fast-paced, constantly evolving business landscape.

Part 1: Understanding Agility
Chapter 1: What is Business Agility?

In today's fast-paced, ever-changing business landscape, the concept of agility has become more important than ever.

But what exactly do we mean by "business agility"?

At its core, business agility is the ability of an organization to rapidly adapt and respond to changes in the market, customer needs, and internal challenges. It's about being flexible, nimble, and proactive in the face of uncertainty and complexity.

As the Agile Alliance defines it, "Agile is a set of methods and practices where solutions evolve through collaboration between self-organizing, cross-functional teams."

While agile practices originated in the software development world, the principles and mindset have since been applied to all aspects of business, from strategy and operations to marketing and HR. The need for business agility has never been more pressing.

In a survey by the Economist, many companies reported that the COVID-19 pandemic forced them to embrace agility in ways they had never done before. Remote work and a scattered workplace altered the balance of power between employees and management, requiring greater trust, transparency, and flexibility.

But even before the pandemic, the pace of change in business was accelerating at an unprecedented rate.

Disruptive technologies, shifting consumer preferences, and global competition have made it impossible for companies to rely on static plans and rigid hierarchies. As Jim Collins, author of the seminal book "Good to Great," puts it: "No one has the right to whine about their company, their industry, or the kind of business that they're in—never again."

So what does it take to achieve true business agility?

According to a report by ProjectManager, there are three fundamental elements of a business agility framework:

1. *Lean execution:* Responding immediately to feedback without sacrificing quality.

2. *Organizational learning:* Rapidly organizing and learning from experience.

3. *Customer experience:* Delivering a great customer experience through agility.

Achieving these elements requires a fundamental shift in mindset and culture.

Agile organizations prioritize outcomes over outputs, collaboration over silos, and experimentation over perfection. They empower teams to make decisions autonomously, while providing the necessary support and guidance to ensure alignment with overall business goals.

Of course, becoming an agile organization is easier said than done.

The 17th Annual State of Agile Report cites several common barriers to agility, including resistance to change, lack of leadership support, and inconsistent processes across teams. Overcoming these challenges requires a clear vision, strong communication, and a willingness to embrace failure as a learning opportunity.

One key best practice for driving agility is to *"agree on and reinforce your why(s)."*

This means clearly articulating the goals and benefits of agility, setting measurable KPIs, and ensuring that all teams and departments are aligned around these objectives. Without a shared sense of purpose, agile transformations can quickly lose momentum and fall victim to skepticism and resistance.

Another critical factor is **leadership.**

Agile leaders step back and let their teams figure out how to deliver value, but they also step in when teams are unable to resolve issues on their own. They create an environment of psychological safety, where employees feel empowered to take risks, voice dissenting opinions, and learn from their mistakes.

Ultimately, the goal of business agility is to achieve valuable outcomes for customers and success for the business, through highly engaged people.

As Lynne Cazaly illustrates in her simple but powerful quadrant model, the sweet spot is where customer outcomes and employee engagement intersect. When teams are motivated by a sense of purpose and empowered to tap into their expertise, they are more likely to deliver innovative solutions that delight customers and drive business results.

Of course, becoming an agile organization is a journey, not a destination. It requires ongoing experimentation, learning, and adaptation. But for companies that embrace the challenge, the rewards can be immense. Agile organizations are better equipped to navigate uncertainty, seize new opportunities, and create lasting value for all stakeholders.

So as you embark on your own agile journey, remember the words of Jim Collins: "Greatness is not a function of circumstance. Greatness, it turns out, is largely a matter of conscious choice and discipline."

By choosing to embrace agility and committing to the hard work of transformation, you too can unlock the full potential of your organization and thrive in an increasingly complex and rapidly changing world.

Definition and Core Principles

Now that we've explored the high-level concept of business agility, let's dive deeper into its definition and core principles.

At its essence, business agility is the ability of an organization to sense and respond to change in order to deliver value to its customers. It's about being adaptive, flexible, and resilient in the face of uncertainty and complexity.

But what does this look like in practice?

According to the Agile Alliance, there are four core values that underpin agile practices:

1. **Individuals and interactions** over processes and tools

2. **Working software** over comprehensive documentation

3. **Customer collaboration** over contract negotiation

4. **Responding to change** over following a plan

These values emphasize the importance of people, collaboration, and adaptability in achieving agility.

They suggest that while processes, documentation, contracts, and plans have their place, they should never come at the expense of delivering value to customers and responding to changing circumstances.

Building on these values, there are several key principles that define agile organizations:

1. **Customer centricity:** Agile organizations are obsessed with delivering value to their customers. They involve customers early and often in the development process, seeking feedback and making adjustments based on real-world data.

2. **Iterative and incremental delivery:** Rather than trying to deliver a perfect product all at once, agile organizations break work down into smaller, manageable chunks that can be delivered incrementally. This allows them to test and validate ideas quickly, gather feedback, and make course corrections along the way.

3. *Cross-functional collaboration:* Agile organizations break down silos and encourage collaboration across teams and departments. They recognize that complex problems require diverse perspectives and skills, and they foster a culture of transparency, trust, and shared ownership.

4. *Continuous learning and improvement:* Agile organizations embrace a mindset of continuous learning and improvement. They conduct regular retrospectives to reflect on what's working well and what could be improved, and they use data and metrics to guide their decision-making.

5. *Adaptability and flexibility:* Agile organizations are designed to be adaptable and flexible in the face of change. They have flat, networked structures that allow for rapid decision-making and course correction, and they empower teams to experiment and take calculated risks.

At Grazing Minds, we've distilled these principles into our own unique mantra: *"The 3 C's of Agility."*

These are:

1. *Curiosity*: Continuously seeking new insights, perspectives, and opportunities.

2. *Courage:* Taking calculated risks, challenging the status quo, and learning from failure.

3. *Collaboration:* Breaking down silos, fostering trust, and leveraging diverse skills and perspectives.

We believe that by embracing these "3 C's," organizations can unlock the full potential of agility and thrive in an increasingly uncertain and rapidly changing world.

Curiosity drives continuous learning and improvement, courage enables adaptability and innovation, and collaboration powers customer centricity and incremental delivery.

Of course, putting these principles into practice is no easy feat.

It requires a fundamental shift in mindset and culture, as well as a willingness to let go of long-held assumptions and practices. But for organizations that are willing to embrace the challenge, the benefits can be immense.

Take the example of Spotify, which has become a poster child for agile transformation. The music streaming giant has organized itself into small, autonomous teams called "squads" that are responsible for specific features or areas of the product. These squads operate with a high degree of autonomy, allowing them to experiment, iterate, and deliver value to customers quickly.

At the same time, Spotify has fostered a culture of collaboration and continuous learning through its "guild" system, which brings together employees with similar skills and interests to share knowledge and best practices across the organization. This approach has allowed Spotify to balance the benefits of autonomy and alignment, and to continuously evolve its product and business model in response to changing customer needs and market conditions.

Another example is Amazon, which has embraced agility through its "two-pizza team" approach. The idea is that no team should be larger than can be fed by two pizzas, ensuring that teams remain small, focused, and nimble. These teams are given a high degree of autonomy to experiment and innovate, while still being held accountable for delivering value to customers.

At the heart of Amazon's approach is a relentless focus on customer obsession. Teams are encouraged to start with the customer and work backwards, using data and insights to continuously improve the customer experience. This customer-centric mindset has allowed Amazon to expand beyond its roots as an online bookstore to become a global leader in e-commerce, cloud computing, and artificial intelligence.

Of course, embracing agility is not without its challenges.

It requires a willingness to embrace uncertainty, to take calculated risks, and to learn from failure. It also requires a deep commitment to continuous learning and improvement, and a recognition that agility is a journey, not a destination.

But for organizations that are willing to embrace the challenge, the rewards can be significant. By becoming more agile, organizations can improve their ability to sense and respond to change, deliver value to customers more quickly and effectively, and foster a culture of innovation and continuous improvement.

So as you embark on your own agile journey, remember the "3 C's" of agility: curiosity, courage, and collaboration.

By embracing these principles and putting them into practice, you too can unlock the full potential of your organization and thrive in an increasingly complex and rapidly changing world.

Agility vs. Traditional Approaches

Now that we've defined business agility and explored its core principles, let's take a closer look at how it differs from traditional approaches to management and organizational design.

While agility has gained widespread adoption in recent years, many organizations still operate based on long-held assumptions and practices that can hinder their ability to adapt and respond to change.

At its core, *the traditional approach to management is based on a hierarchical, command-and-control model.*

Decisions are made at the top and cascaded down through the organization, with each layer of management responsible for overseeing the work of those below them. This approach assumes that leaders have all the answers and that employees are there to execute on their directives.

In contrast, ***agility is based on a more networked, decentralized model.***

Decisions are made as close to the customer as possible, with teams empowered to experiment, learn, and adapt based on real-world feedback. Leaders act more as coaches and facilitators, providing guidance and support rather than micromanaging every aspect of the work.

One of the key differences between agility and traditional approaches is the focus on outcomes over outputs.

Traditional organizations tend to measure success based on adherence to plans and processes, with a focus on delivering specific outputs on time and on budget. Agile organizations, on the other hand, prioritize outcomes over outputs, recognizing that plans and processes are merely means to an end.

This focus on outcomes requires a fundamental shift in mindset and culture.

Rather than trying to predict and control every aspect of the work, agile organizations embrace uncertainty and change as opportunities to learn and adapt. They recognize that the path to success is rarely a straight line, and that the best way to navigate complexity is through rapid experimentation and iteration.

Another key difference is the ***emphasis on cross-functional collaboration over functional silos.***

Traditional organizations tend to be organized around functional departments, with each department responsible for a specific area of expertise. This approach can lead to silos and inefficiencies, as each department optimizes for its own goals rather than the overall needs of the customer.

Agile organizations, in contrast, organize around cross-functional teams that bring together diverse skills and perspectives to solve complex problems. These teams are empowered to make decisions and take ownership of their work, with a focus on delivering value to the customer rather than adhering to rigid functional boundaries.

This approach requires a deep commitment to collaboration and communication. Agile teams work closely together, using practices like daily stand-ups, retrospectives, and co-location to foster transparency, trust, and shared ownership. They recognize that the best ideas often emerge from the intersection of different perspectives and experiences, and that the key to success is creating an environment where everyone feels empowered to contribute.

Of course, shifting from a traditional to an agile approach is no easy feat.

It requires a willingness to challenge long-held assumptions and practices, and to embrace a mindset of continuous learning and improvement. It also requires a deep commitment from leadership to model the behaviours and values of agility, and to create an environment where experimentation and risk-taking are encouraged.

But for organizations that are willing to make the shift, the benefits can be significant.

Agile organizations are better equipped to sense and respond to changing customer needs and market conditions, to deliver value more quickly and effectively, and to foster a culture of innovation and engagement.

One powerful example of this shift is the transformation of ING, the Dutch banking giant.

In 2015, ING embarked on an ambitious agile transformation, reorganizing its 3,500-person headquarters into cross-functional "squads" and "tribes" focused on delivering value to customers.

The results were impressive: time-to-market accelerated from months to weeks, employee engagement increased by 20%, and customer satisfaction scores rose by 10 points.

Another example is the US Department of Defense, which has embraced agility as a way to keep pace with rapidly evolving threats and technologies.

The DoD has created a new "Defense Innovation Board" to bring together experts from industry, academia, and government to help drive agile transformation across the military. By embracing practices like rapid prototyping, user-centered design, and continuous delivery, the DoD hopes to become more responsive, resilient, and effective in the face of an increasingly complex and uncertain world.

Of course, embracing agility is not a one-size-fits-all proposition.

Each organization must find its own path based on its unique context, culture, and goals. But by embracing the core principles of agility - customer centricity, iterative delivery, cross-functional collaboration, continuous learning, and adaptability - organizations can unlock new levels of innovation, engagement, and success.

So as you consider your own organization's approach to management and organizational design, ask yourself: ***are we optimizing for outputs or outcomes?***

◈ Are we fostering silos or collaboration?

◈ Are we clinging to long-held assumptions or embracing a mindset of continuous learning and improvement?

By honestly assessing your current state and identifying opportunities for growth, you can begin to chart a course towards greater agility and success.

At Grazing Minds, we've seen firsthand the power of agility to transform organizations and unlock new levels of potential. By embracing the "3 C's" of curiosity, courage, and collaboration, we've been able to navigate complex challenges, deliver value to our customers more quickly and effectively, and foster a culture of innovation and engagement.

And we believe that by sharing our experiences and insights with others, we can help more organizations embrace the power of agility and thrive in an increasingly uncertain and rapidly changing world.

Exercise: Assess Your Organization's Agile Maturity

Take a few minutes to reflect on your organization's current level of agile maturity. Consider the following questions:

1. How well does your organization respond to changes in the market, customer needs, and internal challenges?

2. To what extent are teams empowered to make decisions autonomously and experiment with new ideas?

3. How effectively does your organization learn from experience and adapt its processes and practices accordingly?

4. How well does your organization deliver value to customers through agility?

5. What are the biggest barriers to agility in your organization, and how might you overcome them?

Chapter 2: The Agile Mindset

In the previous chapter, we explored the definition and core principles of business agility, and how it differs from traditional approaches to management and organizational design. But to truly embrace agility, it's not enough to simply adopt new practices and processes. Rather, it requires a fundamental shift in mindset and culture, one that prioritizes adaptability, collaboration, and continuous learning.

At the heart of this shift is what we call the ***"agile mindset."***

This mindset is characterized by a set of values, beliefs, and attitudes that enable individuals and organizations to thrive in the face of uncertainty and change. It's a way of thinking and being that emphasizes flexibility, experimentation, and a willingness to learn from failure.

One of the key elements of the agile mindset is *a focus on delivering value to customers.*

Rather than getting bogged down in internal processes and politics, agile organizations are obsessed with understanding and meeting the needs of their customers. They involve customers early and often in the development process, seeking feedback and making adjustments based on real-world data.

This customer-centric approach requires a deep empathy and a willingness to put oneself in the customer's shoes. Agile teams use practices like user story mapping, customer interviews, and usability testing to gain a deep understanding of customer needs and preferences. They recognize that the best way to deliver value is to start with the customer and work backwards, rather than trying to impose a predetermined solution.

Another key element of the agile mindset *is a bias towards action and experimentation.*

Rather than getting paralysed by uncertainty or the fear of failure, agile teams embrace a "fail fast, learn faster" approach. They recognize that the path to success is often paved with small, incremental experiments that allow them to test and validate ideas quickly.

This approach requires a willingness to take calculated risks and to view failure as an opportunity to learn and improve.

Agile teams use practices like minimum viable products (MVPs), A/B testing, and continuous delivery to rapidly prototype and test new ideas. They measure success based on real-world outcomes rather than adherence to plans or processes.

A third element of the agile mindset *is a commitment to continuous learning and improvement.*

Agile organizations recognize that in a rapidly changing world, the only sustainable competitive advantage is the ability to learn and adapt faster than the competition. They foster a culture of curiosity, experimentation, and reflection, one that values growth and development over perfection.

This learning mindset is embodied in practices like retrospectives, where teams regularly reflect on what's working well and what could be improved. It's also reflected in a willingness to embrace feedback and constructive criticism, and to see challenges as opportunities for growth and development.

Of course, cultivating an agile mindset is easier said than done.

It requires a willingness to let go of long-held assumptions and practices, and to embrace a new way of working that can feel unfamiliar and uncomfortable at first. It also requires a deep commitment from leadership to model the behaviours and values of agility, and to create an environment where experimentation and risk-taking are encouraged.

One powerful example of the agile mindset in action is the story of Intuit.

In the early 2000s, Intuit was facing increasing competition from web-based startups and struggling to keep pace with the rapid changes in technology and customer expectations.

To respond to these challenges, Intuit embarked on a journey to become a more agile and innovative organization.

They began by embracing a customer-centric approach, using design thinking and rapid experimentation to deeply understand and meet the needs of their customers. They also fostered a culture of experimentation and risk-taking, encouraging employees to propose and test new ideas through a program called "Design for Delight."

Over time, these efforts paid off in a big way!!

Intuit was able to accelerate its innovation cycle, launching new products and features more quickly and effectively than ever before. They also saw significant improvements in employee engagement and customer satisfaction, with Net Promoter Scores rising by double digits.

Another example of the agile mindset in action is the story of Buurtzorg, a Dutch home healthcare organization.

Buurtzorg was founded on the principles of self-management and patient-centred care, with small teams of nurses empowered to make decisions and coordinate care based on the needs of their patients.

This approach required a deep trust in the expertise and judgment of frontline employees, as well as a willingness to let go of traditional hierarchies and control mechanisms. But it also unleashed a wave of innovation and creativity, as teams were able to experiment with new approaches and adapt to the unique needs of each patient.

The results were striking.

Buurtzorg was able to deliver high-quality care at a lower cost than traditional home healthcare organizations, while also achieving high levels of patient and employee satisfaction. Their model has since been studied and replicated around the world, inspiring a new generation of agile and empowered healthcare organizations.

Of course, cultivating an agile mindset is an ongoing journey, not a destination.

It requires a willingness to continuously learn, adapt, and grow, even in the face of setbacks and challenges. But for organizations that are willing to embrace this mindset, the rewards can be significant.

By fostering a culture of curiosity, experimentation, and customer-centricity, agile organizations are better equipped to navigate the complexities and uncertainties of the modern world. They are able to sense and respond to changing market conditions, to deliver value to customers more quickly and effectively, and to unleash the full potential of their people.

So as you consider your own organization's mindset and culture, ask yourself:

> → Are we truly putting the customer at the centre of everything we do?

> → Are we embracing experimentation and risk-taking as a way to learn and grow?

> → Are we fostering a culture of continuous learning and improvement?

By honestly assessing your current state and identifying opportunities for growth, you can begin to cultivate a more agile and adaptive mindset, one that will serve you well in the face of whatever challenges and opportunities the future may bring.

Cultivating an Agile Culture

Having explored the agile mindset and its key elements, let's now turn our attention to the question of how to cultivate an agile culture within an organization.

While adopting agile practices and processes is important, it's not enough on its own. To truly reap the benefits of agility, organizations must create an environment that supports and reinforces agile values and behaviours.

At its core, an agile culture is one that prioritizes flexibility, collaboration, and continuous learning.

It's a culture that empowers individuals and teams to take ownership of their work, to experiment and take risks, and to adapt to changing circumstances. It's also a culture that values diversity and inclusion, recognizing that the best ideas often emerge from the intersection of different perspectives and experiences.

So what does it take to cultivate an agile culture?

Here are a few key strategies and practices:

1. Lead by example: Agile leadership is critical to creating an agile culture. Leaders must model the behaviors and values of agility, such as transparency, collaboration, and a willingness to learn from failure. They must also create an environment of psychological safety, where individuals feel empowered to take risks and voice their opinions without fear of retribution.

2. Empower teams: Agile organizations are built around empowered, self-organizing teams. This means giving teams the autonomy and resources they need to make decisions and take ownership of their work. It also means breaking down silos and fostering cross-functional collaboration, so that teams can leverage diverse skills and perspectives to solve complex problems.

3. Embrace experimentation: Agile cultures are ones that embrace experimentation and risk-taking. This means creating space for teams to try new things, even if they don't always succeed. It also means celebrating learning and growth, rather than just focusing on success or failure.

4. Foster continuous learning: Agile cultures prioritize continuous learning and improvement. This means investing in training and development opportunities, as well as creating forums for knowledge sharing and best practice exchange. It also means conducting regular retrospectives and seeking feedback from customers and stakeholders to identify areas for improvement.

5. Align around purpose: Agile cultures are purpose-driven, with a clear sense of mission and values that guide decision-making and behaviour. This means taking the time to articulate and communicate a compelling vision for the organization, and ensuring that everyone understands how their work contributes to that vision.

Of course, cultivating an agile culture is not without its challenges.

Here are a few common problems that organizations may encounter, along with some strategies for overcoming them:

Problem 1: Resistance to change

One of the biggest obstacles to creating an agile culture is resistance to change. People may be comfortable with the status quo and reluctant to embrace new ways of working, especially if they perceive them as risky or unfamiliar.

When General Electric (GE) embarked on an agile transformation in the early 2010s, they encountered significant resistance from some parts of the organization. Many employees were skeptical of the new approach and worried about how it would impact their roles and responsibilities.

To overcome this resistance, GE invested heavily in communication and education. They created a comprehensive training program to help employees understand the benefits of agility and how it would be implemented across the organization. They also engaged in extensive stakeholder outreach to build buy-in and address concerns.

Problem 2: Lack of alignment

Another common challenge is lack of alignment around agile values and practices. If different parts of the organization are working towards different goals or using different methodologies, it can create confusion and inefficiency.

When Adobe embarked on an agile transformation, they initially struggled with alignment across different teams and departments. Some teams were using Scrum, while others were using Kanban or other methodologies, leading to inconsistency and miscommunication.

To address this challenge, Adobe created a centralized Agile Center of Excellence (ACE) to provide guidance and support to teams across the organization. The ACE team worked to standardize agile practices and tools, while also allowing for flexibility and customization based on team needs.

Problem 3: Overemphasis on process

A third challenge is the tendency to overemphasize process at the expense of people and outcomes. While agile practices and tools are important, they should not be treated as ends in themselves.

When Cisco Systems adopted agile practices in the early 2010s, some teams became overly focused on following the "rules" of Scrum or other methodologies, rather than adapting them to their specific context and needs. This led to a rigid and inflexible approach that stifled innovation and creativity.

To overcome this challenge, Cisco encouraged teams to experiment and adapt agile practices based on their unique needs and goals. They also emphasized the importance of collaboration, communication, and continuous learning, rather than just following a set process.

Cultivating an agile culture is an ongoing journey that requires patience, persistence, and a willingness to learn and adapt.

But for organizations that are willing to invest in the hard work of cultural transformation, the rewards can be significant.

By creating an environment that supports and reinforces agile values and behaviours, organizations can unlock new levels of innovation, engagement, and customer value. They can also become more resilient and adaptable in the face of change and uncertainty, which is increasingly essential in today's fast-paced and unpredictable business landscape.

Leadership Traits for Fostering Agility

As we've seen, cultivating an agile culture requires more than just adopting new practices and processes. It also requires a fundamental shift in leadership mindset and behaviour.

Agile leaders are those who embody the values and principles of agility, and who create an environment that empowers and enables their teams to do their best work.

So what does agile leadership look like in practice?

Here are some key traits and behaviours that are essential for fostering agility:

1. Visionary: Agile leaders are visionary, with a clear sense of purpose and direction. They are able to articulate a compelling vision for the future, and inspire others to work towards that vision. They also have the courage to challenge the status quo and take risks in pursuit of new opportunities.

When Satya Nadella took over as CEO of Microsoft in 2014, he set a new vision for the company around cloud computing and artificial intelligence. He also made bold bets on new technologies and business models, such as the acquisition of LinkedIn and the launch of the Azure cloud platform. These moves helped to reposition Microsoft as a leader in the digital economy.

2. Empowering: Agile leaders empower their teams to take ownership and make decisions. They provide clear goals and guidelines, but trust their teams to figure out the best way to achieve those goals. They also create an environment of psychological safety, where people feel comfortable taking risks and learning from failure.

When ANZ Bank embarked on an agile transformation in 2017, they made a conscious effort to empower their teams and reduce hierarchy. They created cross-functional "squads" that were given the autonomy to make decisions and deliver value to customers. They also invested in coaching and training to help leaders develop a more empowering and collaborative leadership style.

3. Adaptive: Agile leaders are adaptive and flexible, able to navigate change and uncertainty with ease. They are comfortable with ambiguity and are able to pivot quickly in response to new information or changing circumstances. They also encourage their teams to experiment and iterate, rather than sticking rigidly to a plan.

When the COVID-19 pandemic hit in 2020, many organizations had to quickly adapt to new ways of working. One company that did this particularly well was Zoom, the video conferencing platform. Zoom's leadership team was able to rapidly scale up their infrastructure and support to meet the sudden surge in demand, while also rolling out new features and security enhancements to address customer needs.

4. Collaborative: Agile leaders are collaborative and inclusive, able to bring together diverse teams and stakeholders to solve complex problems. They foster a culture of open communication and knowledge sharing, and actively seek out different perspectives and ideas. They also model collaboration in their own behaviour, working closely with other leaders and teams across the organization.

When ING embarked on their agile transformation in 2015, they made collaboration a key focus. They created cross-functional "squads" and "tribes" that brought together people from different parts of the organization to work on shared goals. They also invested in new collaboration tools and spaces, such as open-plan offices and digital whiteboards, to facilitate teamwork and knowledge sharing.

5. Continuous learner: Finally, agile leaders are continuous learners, always seeking out new knowledge and skills. They are curious and open-minded, and encourage their teams to experiment and learn from both successes and failures. They also invest in their own development, attending training and conferences, reading widely, and seeking out mentorship and feedback.

When Pixar Studios was acquired by Disney in 2006, there were concerns that the studio's unique culture of creativity and innovation would be lost. However, under the leadership of Ed Catmull and John Lasseter, Pixar was able to maintain its commitment to continuous learning and improvement. They invested heavily in employee development, offering classes and workshops on everything from storytelling to computer animation. They also created a culture of "plussing," where everyone was encouraged to build on and improve each other's ideas.

Of course, developing these leadership traits and behaviours is not always easy and easier said than done.

It requires a willingness to let go of old habits and assumptions, and to embrace a new way of thinking and working. It also requires a deep commitment to personal and professional growth, and a willingness to lead by example.

But for leaders who are willing to make this shift, the benefits can be significant.

By fostering a culture of agility and empowerment, they can unlock new levels of innovation, engagement, and performance. They can also create organizations that are more resilient and adaptable in the face of change and uncertainty.

So as you consider your own leadership style and approach,

ask yourself:

> → Am I creating a vision and inspiring others to work towards it?

> → Am I empowering my teams to take ownership and make decisions?

→ Am I modeling collaboration and inclusivity in my own behavior?

→ Am I continuously learning and growing, and encouraging others to do the same?

By honestly assessing your strengths and areas for improvement, and committing to ongoing development and growth, you can become the kind of leader that fosters agility and drives success in today's fast-paced and ever-changing business landscape.

It won't be easy, but the rewards - for you, your team, and your organization - will be well worth the effort.

Activity : Agility in Action: A Team-Based Simulation

Objective:

To experience the benefits of agility firsthand and develop a deeper understanding of the agile mindset and culture through a team-based simulation activity.

Instructions:

1. Form teams of 4-6 people. If you're doing this activity within your organization, try to create cross-functional teams with members from different departments or areas of expertise.

2. Choose a real-world business challenge or opportunity that your organization is currently facing. It could be anything from improving customer satisfaction to launching a new product or service.

3. As a team, spend 15-20 minutes brainstorming potential solutions or approaches to the challenge. Encourage everyone to share their ideas freely, without judgment or criticism.

4. Next, select one of the ideas to prototype and test. Using whatever materials you have available (e.g., paper, markers, sticky notes), create a rough prototype or mockup of your solution. Don't worry about making it perfect - the goal is to quickly visualize and communicate your idea.

5. Once your prototype is ready, present it to another team or group of stakeholders. Explain your thinking and rationale, and gather feedback and suggestions for improvement.

6. Based on the feedback you receive, spend another 10-15 minutes iterating and refining your prototype. Look for ways to incorporate new ideas or address any concerns or limitations that were raised.

7. Present your updated prototype to the same group as before, and gather additional feedback. Repeat the iteration process as many times as possible within the allotted timeframe.

8. At the end of the activity, come together as a group to debrief and reflect on the experience. Some questions to consider:

- What did you learn about the agile mindset and culture through this activity?

- How did the iterative process of prototyping and gathering feedback help you improve your solution?

- What challenges or obstacles did you encounter along the way, and how did you overcome them?

- How might you apply these lessons to your own work or projects?

Tips for Success:

- Encourage a spirit of experimentation and risk-taking throughout the activity.

Emphasize that there are no "right" or "wrong" answers, and that the goal is to learn and improve through iteration.

- Foster a culture of collaboration and communication within your team.

Make sure everyone has a chance to contribute their ideas and perspectives, and actively seek out feedback and input from others.

- Embrace failure as an opportunity to learn and grow.

If an idea doesn't work out as planned, don't get discouraged - instead, use it as a chance to pivot and try something new.

- Have fun and be creative!

This activity is a chance to step outside your normal roles and routines and explore new possibilities. Embrace the opportunity to think differently and approach challenges in a fresh way.

By participating in this simulation activity, readers will have a chance to experience the agile mindset and culture in action, and gain practical insights and skills that they can apply to their own work and leadership.

It's a fun and engaging way to bring the concepts from Chapters 1 and 2 to life, and help readers develop a deeper understanding of what it takes to foster agility and drive success in today's fast-paced and ever-changing business landscape.

Chapter 3: Agile Frameworks and Methodologies

In the previous chapters, we explored the agile mindset and culture, and the leadership traits necessary for fostering agility within an organization.

Now, let's dive into some of the most popular and effective agile frameworks and methodologies that have emerged in recent years.

While many people are familiar with traditional agile approaches like Scrum and Kanban, there are a number of newer frameworks that have gained traction in recent years due to their ability to address the unique challenges and opportunities of today's business landscape.

In this chapter, we'll explore some of these cutting-edge approaches and how they can help organizations achieve greater agility, innovation, and success.

Scaled Agile Framework (SAFe)

One of the most popular and widely-adopted agile frameworks in recent years is the Scaled Agile Framework, or SAFe. Developed by Dean Leffingwell and his team at Scaled Agile Inc., SAFe is designed to help large organizations scale agile practices across multiple teams and departments.

SAFe is based on a set of core values and principles, including alignment, built-in quality, transparency, and program execution. It provides a structured approach to agile development that includes a set of roles, ceremonies, and artifacts designed to help teams collaborate effectively and deliver value quickly.

One of the key benefits of SAFe is its ability to align teams around a common vision and set of goals.

By creating a shared understanding of the "big picture" and how each team's work fits into it, SAFe helps organizations avoid the pitfalls of siloed thinking and conflicting priorities. One company that has successfully adopted SAFe is Cisco Systems.

In 2015, Cisco began using SAFe to help scale agile practices across its engineering organization, which consists of more than 25,000 people. By creating a common language and set of practices around agile development, Cisco was able to improve collaboration, reduce cycle times, and increase the quality and predictability of its software releases.

Large-Scale Scrum (LeSS)

Another popular framework for scaling agile practices is Large-Scale Scrum, or LeSS. Developed by Craig Larman and Bas Vodde, LeSS is designed to help organizations apply the principles and practices of Scrum to large, complex projects.

Like SAFe, LeSS emphasizes the importance of aligning teams around a common goal and creating a shared understanding of the work being done. However, LeSS takes a more minimalist approach than SAFe, with a focus on simplicity and continuous improvement.

One of the key practices in LeSS is the use of "feature teams," which are cross-functional teams that are responsible for delivering end-to-end features rather than individual components or modules.

By organizing teams around features rather than components, LeSS helps organizations reduce dependencies and improve flow. One company that has successfully adopted LeSS is Nokia Networks.

In 2015, Nokia began using LeSS to help scale agile practices across its mobile networks division, which consists of more than 2,000 people. By creating feature teams and emphasizing continuous improvement, Nokia was able to reduce cycle times, improve quality, and increase customer satisfaction.

Disciplined Agile (DA)

A newer entrant to the agile framework landscape is Disciplined Agile, or DA. Developed by Scott Ambler and Mark Lines, DA is a hybrid approach that combines elements of Scrum, Kanban, Lean, and other agile methodologies.

One of the key benefits of DA is its flexibility and adaptability. Rather than prescribing a one-size-fits-all approach, DA provides a toolkit of practices and techniques that teams can choose from based on their specific needs and context.

DA also emphasizes the importance of continuous improvement and learning. Teams are encouraged to experiment with different practices and approaches, and to use feedback and data to continuously optimize their processes and outcomes.

In 2018, the US Department of Veterans Affairs (VA) began using DA to help modernize its software development practices and improve the quality and efficiency of its services to veterans. By adopting a more flexible and adaptive approach to agile development, the VA was able to reduce cycle times, improve collaboration, and deliver better outcomes for its customers.

These are just a few examples of the many agile frameworks and methodologies that have emerged in recent years.

While each approach has its own unique features and benefits, they all share a common goal of helping organizations become more agile, responsive, and customer-focused.

As you consider which framework or methodology might be right for your organization, it's important to keep in mind that there is no one-size-fits-all solution.

The key is to experiment with different approaches, learn from your successes and failures, and continuously adapt and improve over time.

By embracing a spirit of experimentation and learning, and by staying open to new ideas and approaches, you can create an organization that is truly built for agility and success in the years ahead.

Choosing the Right Framework for Your Organization

With so many agile frameworks and methodologies to choose from, it can be challenging to know which one is right for your organization.

While each approach has its own strengths and benefits, the reality is that no single framework is a perfect fit for every context.

Instead of adopting a framework wholesale, many organizations are finding success by creating their own customized approach that borrows elements from multiple frameworks.

By cherry-picking the practices and techniques that work best for their specific needs and culture, these organizations are able to create a tailored approach that maximizes the benefits of agility while minimizing the potential drawbacks.

One way to approach this is by using a "best of breed" strategy, where you identify the key practices and techniques from each framework that are most relevant and valuable for your organization. For example, you might borrow the concept of "feature teams" from LeSS, the emphasis on continuous improvement from DA, and the structured approach to program execution from SAFe.

By combining these elements in a way that makes sense for your organization, you can create a customized framework that is both effective and efficient.

To make this process more manageable, we can use a simple acronym to guide our thinking: ***A.D.A.P.T.***

- **A**ssess your current context and needs

- **D**efine your goals and objectives

- **A**nalyse the available frameworks and methodologies

- **P**ick the practices and techniques that work best for you

- **T**ailor your approach based on feedback and learning

Let's explore each of these steps in more detail:

Assess your current context and needs:

Before you can choose the right framework for your organization, you need to have a clear understanding of your current context and needs. This includes factors like your organizational structure, culture, technology stack, and business objectives. By taking stock of where you are today, you can identify the areas where you need to improve and the challenges you need to overcome.

Define your goals and objectives:

Once you have a clear understanding of your current state, the next step is to define your goals and objectives for adopting an agile approach. What outcomes are you hoping to achieve?

What benefits are you looking to realize? By clarifying your goals upfront, you can ensure that your chosen framework is aligned with your overall strategy and priorities.

Analyse the available frameworks and methodologies:

With your goals and context in mind, the next step is to analyse the available frameworks and methodologies to identify which ones are the best fit for your needs. This may involve doing research, attending training or workshops, or consulting with experts who have experience with different approaches.

Pick the practices and techniques that work best for you:

Based on your analysis, the next step is to pick the specific practices and techniques that you want to adopt from each framework. This might include things like user stories, retrospectives, continuous integration, or value stream mapping. The key is to choose the practices that are most relevant and valuable for your specific context and goals.

Tailor your approach based on feedback and learning:

Finally, as you begin to implement your chosen practices and techniques, it's important to continuously monitor and adapt your approach based on feedback and learning. Agile is all about continuous improvement, so be prepared to experiment, make mistakes, and iterate as you go.

One organization that has successfully used an A.D.A.P.T approach is Spotify.

Rather than adopting a single agile framework wholesale, Spotify has created its own custom approach that borrows elements from Scrum, Kanban, and Lean Startup. This includes practices like autonomous squads, tribes, and guilds, as well as a focus on continuous delivery and experimentation. By tailoring their approach to their specific needs and culture, Spotify has been able to achieve a high degree of agility and innovation, while still maintaining a strong sense of alignment and purpose across the organization.

As you embark on your own agile journey, remember that the key is to stay open to learning and adaptation.

By using the A.D.A.P.T framework as a guide, you can create a customized approach that works best for your organization, and that helps you achieve your goals and objectives in a way that is both effective and sustainable over the long term.

Part 2: Implementing Agility Across Business Functions

Chapter 4: Agile Strategy and Planning

In the previous chapter, we explored some of the most popular and effective agile frameworks and methodologies, and discussed how organizations can choose the right approach for their specific needs and context.

Now, let's dive into the topic of agile strategy and planning, and explore how organizations can create a more adaptive and responsive approach to strategic decision-making.

In today's fast-paced and unpredictable business environment, traditional approaches to strategy and planning are often too slow and inflexible to keep up with the rapid pace of change.

By the time a plan is developed and implemented, the market or competitive landscape may have already shifted, rendering the plan obsolete.

Agile strategy and planning, on the other hand, is all about creating a more dynamic and iterative approach to strategic decision-making.

Rather than trying to predict the future and create a detailed long-term plan, agile organizations focus on creating a clear vision and direction, while remaining flexible and adaptable in the face of change.

One of the key principles of agile strategy and planning is the idea of "*sense and respond*." This means that rather than trying to control or predict the future, organizations need to be constantly sensing and responding to changes in the market, customer needs, and other external factors.

Another key principle is the idea of "*continuous planning*." Rather than creating a single, comprehensive plan that is set in stone, agile organizations engage in ongoing planning and adaptation based on feedback and learning. This might involve regular strategy reviews, frequent iterations on tactics and initiatives, and a willingness to pivot or change course as needed.

One company that has successfully adopted an agile approach to strategy and planning is Netflix. Rather than trying to predict the future of the entertainment industry, Netflix has focused on creating a clear vision and set of values, while remaining flexible and adaptable in the face of change.

This has involved a number of key practices, such as:

- Regular strategy reviews and iterations based on data and feedback

- A focus on experimentation and testing, with a willingness to quickly abandon ideas that don't work

- A decentralized approach to decision-making, with teams empowered to make strategic choices based on their specific context and expertise

- A culture of transparency and collaboration, with information shared openly across the organization

By adopting these practices, Netflix has been able to consistently stay ahead of the curve in an industry that is undergoing rapid disruption and change. They have been able to quickly pivot to new opportunities, such as original content creation and international expansion, while maintaining a strong focus on their core vision and values.

Another example of an organization that has successfully adopted an agile approach to strategy and planning is the US Department of Defense (DoD). In recent years, the DoD has recognized the need to become more agile and adaptive in the face of rapidly evolving threats and challenges.

To address this need, the DoD has adopted a number of agile practices, such as:

- The use of "rapid prototyping" and experimentation to quickly test and iterate on new ideas and technologies

- A focus on "mission command," which empowers teams and individuals to make decisions based on their specific context and expertise

- The adoption of "DevSecOps," which integrates security and operations into the software development process to enable faster and more secure delivery of new capabilities

- A shift towards more modular and interoperable systems, which can be quickly adapted and reconfigured as needed

By adopting these practices, the DoD has been able to become more responsive and effective in the face of rapidly evolving threats and challenges. They have been able to quickly develop and deploy new capabilities, while maintaining a strong focus on security and mission effectiveness.

As you consider how to adopt a more agile approach to strategy and planning in your own organization, there are a few key things to keep in mind:

1. Start with a clear vision and set of values:

Agile strategy and planning is not about abandoning long-term thinking altogether. Rather, it's about creating a clear and compelling vision for the future, while remaining flexible and adaptable in how you get there. Take the time to articulate your organization's core purpose, values, and strategic priorities, and use these as a guidepost for decision-making and adaptation.

2. Embrace experimentation and learning:

Agile strategy and planning is all about continuous learning and improvement. Encourage a culture of experimentation and risk-taking, and create space for teams to test new ideas and approaches. Use data and feedback to continuously refine and adapt your strategy over time.

3. Empower teams and individuals:

Agile organizations rely on the expertise and judgment of their people to make smart, context-specific decisions. Create a culture of trust and empowerment, where teams and individuals are given the autonomy and resources they need to drive strategic initiatives forward.

4. Foster collaboration and transparency:

Agile strategy and planning require a high degree of collaboration and information sharing across the organization. Break down silos and create channels for cross-functional communication and coordination. Use tools and practices like open roadmaps, regular progress reviews, and collaborative planning sessions to keep everyone aligned and informed.

By adopting these practices and mindsets, you can create a more agile and adaptive approach to strategy and planning in your organization.

While it may require a significant shift in thinking and behaviour, the benefits - in terms of increased responsiveness, innovation, and effectiveness - are well worth the effort.

Setting Adaptive Goals and Objectives

One of the key challenges of traditional strategic planning is that it often relies on setting long-term, fixed goals and objectives.

In a rapidly changing business environment, however, these goals can quickly become outdated or irrelevant, leading to wasted effort and missed opportunities.

In an agile approach to strategy and planning, the focus shifts towards setting adaptive goals and objectives that can evolve and change over time based on new information and insights. Rather than trying to predict the future and set a fixed destination, agile organizations focus on creating a clear direction and vision, while remaining open to new possibilities and course corrections along the way.

So, what does this look like in practice?

Here are a few key principles and practices for setting adaptive goals and objectives:

1. Focus on outcomes, not outputs:

Rather than setting goals based on specific deliverables or milestones, focus on the outcomes and benefits you want to achieve. This might include things like customer satisfaction, market share, or employee engagement. By focusing on outcomes, you can create a more flexible and adaptable approach that can evolve as circumstances change.

2. Use short-term, iterative goals:

Rather than setting long-term, annual goals, break them down into shorter-term, iterative objectives that can be regularly reviewed and adapted. This might involve setting quarterly or even monthly goals, with regular check-ins and adjustments based on progress and feedback.

Adobe has adopted an approach called ***"Objectives and Key Results" (OKRs)*** to set and track adaptive goals across the organization.

Each quarter, teams set a small number of high-level objectives, along with specific, measurable key results that indicate progress towards those objectives. These OKRs are regularly reviewed and adapted based on new information and insights, allowing teams to stay aligned and focused while remaining flexible and responsive.

3. Embrace uncertainty and experimentation:

In a fast-changing environment, it's impossible to have all the answers upfront. Instead of trying to create a perfect plan, embrace uncertainty and build experimentation into your goal-setting process. Encourage teams to test new ideas and approaches, and use data and feedback to continuously refine and adapt their goals over time.

Airbnb has a culture of experimentation and data-driven decision making that is reflected in their approach to goal setting. Teams are encouraged to set "stretch goals" that push them outside their comfort zone, and to use data and testing to validate their assumptions and hypotheses. This has allowed Airbnb to quickly adapt to changing market conditions and customer needs, while maintaining a strong focus on their core mission and values.

4. Align goals across the organization:

While agile goal setting emphasizes flexibility and adaptation, it's still important to create alignment and coherence across the organization. Make sure that team-level goals are aligned with overall strategic priorities, and that there are mechanisms in place for cross-functional coordination and collaboration.

Spotify has a unique approach to goal setting that emphasizes alignment and autonomy. Teams are organized into "squads" that are responsible for specific features or capabilities, and are given the freedom to set their own goals and priorities. However, these goals are aligned with higher-level "missions" and "bets" that are set at the company level, ensuring that everyone is working towards a common vision and direction.

5. Celebrate learning and adaptation:

Finally, it's important to create a culture that celebrates learning and adaptation, rather than just hitting fixed targets. Recognize and reward teams for their ability to experiment, learn, and adjust their goals based on new insights and information. This can help to create a more resilient and innovative organization that is better equipped to thrive in a rapidly changing world.

By adopting these principles and practices, you can create a more adaptive and responsive approach to goal setting in your organization. While it may require a shift in mindset and behaviour, the benefits - in terms of increased agility, innovation, and resilience - are well worth the effort.

As you embark on this journey, remember that setting adaptive goals is not a one-time event, but an ongoing process of learning and iteration.

Encourage teams to regularly review and adjust their goals based on new information and insights, and create a culture that values experimentation and continuous improvement.

By doing so, you can create an organization that is better equipped to navigate the challenges and opportunities of a rapidly changing world, and to deliver value to customers and stakeholders in a more agile and responsive way.

Conducting Agile Strategic Planning Sessions

Agile strategic planning sessions are a key component of creating an adaptive and responsive approach to strategy and planning.

These sessions bring together key stakeholders and decision-makers to set direction, align on priorities, and make critical decisions in a fast-paced and collaborative environment.

However, conducting effective agile strategic planning sessions requires a different approach than traditional, linear planning processes.

Here are some key principles and practices to keep in mind:

1. Emphasize collaboration and participation:

Agile strategic planning sessions should be highly collaborative and participatory, with a focus on engaging a diverse range of stakeholders and perspectives. Encourage active participation and create a safe space for open and honest dialogue.

Zappos, the online shoe and clothing retailer, is known for its highly collaborative and inclusive approach to strategic planning. The company regularly brings together employees from across the organization for "all-hands" meetings and strategy sessions, where everyone has a voice and a role in shaping the company's direction and priorities.

2. Use visual and interactive tools:

Agile strategic planning sessions often use visual and interactive tools to facilitate collaboration and alignment. This might include things like whiteboards, sticky notes, or digital collaboration platforms. By making the planning process more visual and tactile, you can create a more engaging and productive environment.

Atlassian, the software company behind products like Jira and Trello, uses a visual and interactive approach to strategic planning called "Play." This involves bringing together cross-functional teams for intensive, multi-day sessions where they use a variety of visual and interactive tools to explore new ideas, set priorities, and align on key initiatives.

3. Focus on outcomes and value:

Agile strategic planning sessions should be focused on identifying and prioritizing the outcomes and value that the organization wants to create, rather than just the specific activities or deliverables. Encourage teams to think in terms of customer needs, business impact, and strategic fit, and to prioritize initiatives based on their potential to deliver value.

Amazon is known for its relentless focus on customer value in its strategic planning and decision making. The company uses a variety of tools and frameworks, such as the "working backwards" process and the "PR/FAQ" document, to ensure that all initiatives are grounded in a deep understanding of customer needs and preferences.

4. Timeboxing and iterative planning:

Agile strategic planning sessions often use timeboxing and iterative planning to create a sense of urgency and focus. This might involve breaking the session into shorter, focused sprints, with clear goals and deliverables for each sprint. Teams can then iterate and adjust their plans based on new information and feedback.

Twitter uses a timeboxed and iterative approach to strategic planning called "Flocks." These are short-term, cross-functional teams that come together for focused sprints to tackle specific strategic initiatives or challenges. Flocks are given clear goals and deliverables, and are empowered to make decisions and adjust their plans based on new information and insights.

5. Foster a culture of experimentation and learning:

Finally, agile strategic planning sessions should foster a culture of experimentation and learning, where teams are encouraged to test new ideas and approaches, and to learn from both successes and failures. Create a safe space for risk-taking and innovation, and celebrate learning and adaptation as key drivers of strategic success.

Intuit, the financial software company behind products like QuickBooks and TurboTax, has a culture of experimentation and learning that is deeply embedded in its strategic planning process. The company uses a variety of tools and frameworks, such as "lean startup" principles and "design thinking," to encourage teams to test new ideas and learn from customer feedback. This has allowed Intuit to continuously evolve and adapt its products and services to meet changing customer needs and preferences.

By adopting these principles and practices, you can create more effective and impactful agile strategic planning sessions in your organization.

Remember that the goal is not just to create a plan, but to foster a culture of collaboration, experimentation, and continuous learning that can help your organization thrive in a rapidly changing world.

As you design and facilitate these sessions, be sure to create a clear agenda and set of objectives, and to engage a diverse range of stakeholders and perspectives. Use visual and interactive tools to facilitate collaboration and alignment, and create a safe space for open and honest dialogue.

Most importantly, remember that agile strategic planning is not a one-time event, but an ongoing process of learning and adaptation.

Encourage teams to regularly review and adjust their plans based on new information and insights, and to celebrate the progress and learning along the way.

By doing so, you can create an organization that is better equipped to navigate the challenges and opportunities of a rapidly changing world, and to deliver value to customers and stakeholders in a more agile and responsive way.

53

Activity: Strategy Safari

Objective:

To encourage participants to look at their organization's strategy from multiple new perspectives, and generate fresh insights and ideas.

Instructions:

1. Divide participants into teams of 4-6 people, ideally from different functions and levels of the organization.

2. Assign each team a different "safari persona" to embody during the activity. For example:

- Customer explorer: Look at the strategy through the eyes of a customer.

- Competitor spy: Analyze the strategy as if you were a competitor.

- Future forecaster: Imagine you are visiting from 10 years in the future.

- Ecosystem mapper: Examine the strategy from the perspective of key partners and stakeholders.

- Sustainability advocate: Evaluate the strategy's environmental and social impact.

3. Give each team 30 minutes to "go on safari" and explore the organization's current strategy from their assigned perspective.

Encourage them to use creative techniques like roleplaying, storytelling, and visual mapping to bring their insights to life.

4. Have each team report back on their safari experience, sharing their key insights and observations. Encourage them to focus on new opportunities, challenges, and blind spots they discovered.

5. As a group, discuss the common themes and surprising differences that emerged across the different perspectives. Brainstorm how these insights could be used to improve or transform the current strategy.

6. Wrap up the activity by having each participant share one concrete action they will take to bring a new perspective into their day-to-day work.

Debrief questions:

- What was it like to look at the strategy from a completely different viewpoint?

- What new insights or ideas emerged that you hadn't considered before?

- How can we institutionalize this kind of perspective-taking in our regular strategic planning process?

- What other perspectives could we explore to generate even more out-of-the-box thinking?

This "Strategy Safari" activity is a fun and engaging way to push participants out of their usual mental models and generate fresh strategic thinking.

By gamifying the perspective-taking process, it encourages creativity, collaboration, and a spirit of experimentation - all key ingredients of agile strategic planning.

Feel free to adapt and customize this activity to suit your specific context and needs. The key is to make perspective-taking a regular and valued part of your strategic conversations, not just a one-off exercise. By constantly challenging ourselves to see things through new lenses, we can develop more robust and adaptive strategies for navigating an uncertain future.

Chapter 5: Agile Marketing and Sales

Digitally-driven business environment, traditional marketing and sales approaches often struggle to keep up with rapidly evolving customer needs and expectations.

Agile marketing and sales have emerged as a powerful way to address these challenges, by bringing greater flexibility, responsiveness, and customer-centricity to the commercial side of the business.

At its core, agile marketing and sales is about applying the principles and practices of agile development - such as iterative planning, cross-functional collaboration, and continuous learning - to the process of creating and delivering value to customers. By working in short sprints, gathering frequent feedback, and constantly adapting to new insights, agile marketing and sales teams can deliver more relevant, personalized, and engaging customer experiences.

One company that has embraced agile marketing and sales is HubSpot, the inbound marketing and sales platform.

HubSpot has adopted an agile approach to content creation, using a "topic cluster" model to organize and prioritize its content calendar based on customer search behavior and feedback. By focusing on creating valuable, relevant content that addresses real customer needs, HubSpot has been able to dramatically improve its search rankings and lead generation performance.

On the sales side, companies like Salesforce have pioneered the use of agile techniques to improve sales team productivity and effectiveness.

Salesforce's "high velocity sales" methodology emphasizes fast, iterative sales cycles, powered by real-time data and analytics. By using tools like AI-powered lead scoring and personalized email cadences, Salesforce's sales reps can focus their time and energy on the most promising opportunities, while continuously optimizing their approach based on what's working.

However, it's important to recognize that agile marketing and sales may look different depending on the geographic and economic context.

In emerging markets, for example, agile approaches may need to be adapted to account for differences in digital infrastructure, consumer behaviour, and cultural norms.

One interesting example is Jumia, the leading e-commerce platform in Africa. Jumia has had to develop its own agile marketing and sales playbook to navigate the unique challenges of the African market, such as low credit card penetration, limited logistics infrastructure, and high mobile phone usage. By using a combination of online and offline channels, such as mobile money payments and local pickup points, Jumia has been able to rapidly grow its customer base and adapt to changing market conditions.

In China, by contrast, agile marketing and sales often takes on a distinctly social and mobile-first flavour.

Chinese consumers are highly engaged on social media platforms like WeChat and Weibo, and expect brands to provide seamless, personalized experiences across multiple touchpoints. Companies like Xiaomi, the smartphone maker, have used agile techniques to rapidly prototype and launch new products and marketing campaigns based on real-time social media feedback and trends.

As these examples illustrate, agile marketing and sales is not a one-size-fits-all approach, but rather a set of principles and practices that need to be adapted to the specific context and needs of each market. By staying attuned to local customer preferences, cultural norms, and technological trends, agile marketing and sales teams can deliver more relevant, engaging, and effective customer experiences, no matter where in the world they operate.

Some key considerations for leaders looking to implement agile marketing and sales in their organizations include:

1. Foster a culture of experimentation and learning:

Encourage teams to constantly test new ideas and approaches, and to view failures as opportunities for learning and improvement.

2. Break down silos between marketing, sales, and other functions:

Agile marketing and sales require close collaboration and communication across the entire organization, from product development to customer service.

3. Invest in the right tools and technologies:

Agile marketing and sales rely heavily on data and analytics to guide decision making, so it's important to have the right tools in place to track and measure customer behaviour and feedback.

4. Empower teams to make decisions and take ownership:

Agile marketing and sales teams need to be able to move quickly and decisively, without getting bogged down in bureaucracy or red tape.

5. Continuously measure and optimize performance:

Use metrics and KPIs to track the effectiveness of marketing and sales initiatives, and be willing to pivot quickly based on what the data is telling you.

By embracing these principles and practices, organizations can unlock the full potential of agile marketing and sales to drive growth, innovation, and customer loyalty in today's fast-moving business landscape.

As with any agile transformation, it requires a willingness to experiment, learn, and adapt over time - but the rewards can be significant for those who get it right.

Applying Agile Principles to Marketing Campaigns

Agile principles, which originated in software development, have found their way into marketing campaigns, revolutionizing the way companies approach their marketing efforts.

By applying agile methodologies, marketers can create more flexible, responsive, and customer-centric campaigns that deliver better results in today's fast-paced digital landscape.

One of the key principles of agile marketing is to work in short, iterative cycles known as *"sprints."*

Instead of planning and executing lengthy, monolithic campaigns, agile marketers break their work into smaller, more manageable chunks that can be quickly developed, tested, and refined based on real-time customer feedback and data.

An excellent example of this approach in action is the "Stratos" campaign by Red Bull.

In 2012, the energy drink company sponsored Austrian skydiver Felix Baumgartner's record-breaking jump from the stratosphere. Rather than simply promoting the event through traditional channels, Red Bull adopted an agile approach, creating a series of short, engaging videos and social media content that built anticipation and excitement leading up to the jump. By continuously monitoring audience engagement and sentiment, Red Bull was able to optimize its content strategy in real-time, resulting in a massive surge of brand awareness and social media buzz.

Another key principle of agile marketing is cross-functional collaboration.

Agile marketing teams are typically composed of people from various disciplines, such as content creators, data analysts, and social media specialists, who work together closely to develop and execute campaigns. This approach helps break down silos between different marketing functions and ensures that everyone is working towards a common goal.

A great example of this is the "Beauty Squad" campaign by Sephora.

The beauty retailer assembled a cross-functional team of makeup artists, social media influencers, and digital marketers to create a series of tutorial videos and social media content showcasing its products. By leveraging the diverse skills and perspectives of its team members, Sephora was able to create highly engaging, authentic content that resonated with its target audience and drove significant sales growth.

However, it's important to recognize that the application of agile principles to marketing campaigns may vary depending on the geographic and economic context. In some regions, cultural differences, technological constraints, or regulatory requirements may necessitate a different approach.

For example, Chinese consumers expect brands to engage with them in real-time, often through one-on-one conversations or group chats. Companies like Xiaohongshu, a social e-commerce platform, have used agile techniques to quickly respond to user feedback and create targeted, localized content that resonates with Chinese consumers.

In other emerging markets, such as India, agile marketing may need to account for the unique challenges of reaching and engaging with consumers across a vast, fragmented media landscape.

For example, Unilever's "Share The Load" campaign, which promoted gender equality in household chores, used an agile approach to tailor its messaging and content formats to different regional and linguistic audiences across India. By continuously testing and refining its approach based on local feedback and data, Unilever was able to drive significant brand lift and social impact.

As these examples illustrate, applying agile principles to marketing campaigns requires a deep understanding of the local market context and a willingness to adapt and experiment based on real-time feedback and data.

Some key considerations for marketers looking to adopt an agile approach include:

1. Start small and scale up:

Begin by applying agile principles to a single campaign or initiative, and gradually expand to other areas of the marketing organization as you learn and refine your approach.

2. Invest in the right tools and talent:

Agile marketing requires a robust technology stack for data analysis, content creation, and project management, as well as a team with diverse skills and a growth mindset.

3. Foster a culture of experimentation and learning:

Encourage teams to take calculated risks, test new ideas, and learn from both successes and failures. Celebrate the process of continuous improvement.

4. Align with other functions:

Agile marketing works best when it is integrated with other parts of the organization, such as product development, sales, and customer service. Foster cross-functional collaboration and communication.

5. Measure what matters:

Focus on metrics that truly reflect customer value and business impact, rather than vanity metrics or short-term gains. Use data to continuously optimize and refine your approach.

By embracing these principles and practices, marketers can create more agile, responsive, and effective campaigns that deliver real value to customers and the business.

As with any agile transformation, it requires a willingness to challenge the status quo, experiment with new approaches, and continuously learn and adapt over time. But for those who get it right, the rewards can be significant in terms of increased brand engagement, customer loyalty, and business growth.

Iterative and Responsive Sales Approaches

Today sales teams need to be more agile and responsive than ever before.

Buyers are increasingly informed, empowered, and expect a personalized, seamless experience across multiple touchpoints. To meet these expectations, many companies are adopting iterative and responsive sales approaches that prioritize flexibility, collaboration, and continuous improvement.

At the core of this approach is the idea of *sales sprints.*

Similar to agile marketing campaigns, sales sprints involve breaking down the sales process into shorter, more focused cycles of prospecting, outreach, and closing. By working in sprints, sales teams can quickly test and refine their approach based on real-time feedback and data, rather than following a rigid, linear process.

One company that has successfully implemented this approach is Shopify.

The e-commerce platform provider has adopted a "sales lab" model, where cross-functional teams of sales reps, marketers, and product specialists collaborate to rapidly test and iterate on new sales strategies and tactics. By using data and experimentation to guide their efforts, Shopify's sales teams have been able to significantly improve their conversion rates and revenue growth.

Another key aspect of iterative and responsive sales is the use of personalization and targeting. With the help of advanced analytics and machine learning tools, sales teams can now gain deeper insights into customer behaviour, preferences, and needs. This allows them to tailor their outreach and messaging to specific segments or even individual buyers, improving the relevance and effectiveness of their sales efforts.

An example of this in action is the "account-based marketing" approach used by Snowflake, the cloud data platform provider.

Snowflake's sales team works closely with marketing to identify and target high-value accounts with personalized content and outreach. By using data to inform their sales strategy and continuously refining their approach based on feedback and results, Snowflake has been able to achieve impressive growth and customer retention rates.

However, it's important to recognize that the adoption of iterative and responsive sales approaches may vary depending on the geographic and economic context. In some regions, cultural norms, business practices, or technological constraints may require a different approach.

For example, in Japan, where business relationships are often built on trust and long-term partnerships, sales cycles tend to be longer and more focused on personal interaction. Companies like Rakuten, the Japanese e-commerce giant, have had to adapt their sales approach to account for these cultural differences, emphasizing face-to-face meetings, relationship-building, and a more consultative selling style.

In emerging markets like Brazil, where the business landscape is highly fragmented and complex, iterative and responsive sales approaches may need to account for a wider range of customer segments and channels.

For example, Natura, the Brazilian cosmetics company, has used an agile sales approach to manage its network of over 1 million independent sales consultants across the country. By providing its consultants with digital tools and training, and continuously gathering feedback and data on sales performance, Natura has been able to optimize its sales strategy and maintain its market leadership position.

As these examples illustrate, implementing iterative and responsive sales approaches requires a deep understanding of the local market context and a willingness to adapt and experiment based on real-time feedback and data.

Some key considerations for sales leaders looking to adopt this approach include:

1. Foster a culture of experimentation and learning:

Encourage sales teams to test new ideas, learn from failures, and continuously improve their approach. Celebrate the process of iteration and optimization.

2. Break down silos between sales and other functions:

Iterative and responsive sales require close collaboration with marketing, product, and customer success teams. Foster cross-functional communication and alignment.

3. Invest in the right tools and training:

Provide sales teams with the technology and skills they need to gather and analyse customer data, personalize their outreach, and collaborate effectively.

4. Focus on customer value:

Prioritize sales metrics that reflect customer satisfaction, retention, and lifetime value, rather than just short-term revenue or volume. Use customer feedback to continuously improve the sales experience.

5. Adapt to the local context:

Be aware of the unique cultural, economic, and technological factors that shape sales practices in different regions. Tailor your approach accordingly, while staying true to the core principles of agility and responsiveness.

By embracing these principles and practices, sales teams can become nimbler, customer-centric, and effective in today's fast-changing business landscape.

As with any agile transformation, it requires a willingness to challenge traditional sales models, experiment with new approaches, and continuously learn and adapt over time. But for those who get it right, the rewards can be significant in terms of increased sales productivity, customer loyalty, and business growth.

Chapter 6: Agile Operations and Supply Chain Management

———

In the fast-paced, ever-changing business landscape, companies are increasingly turning to agile principles to transform their operations and supply chain management. By embracing flexibility, responsiveness, and continuous improvement, organizations can better navigate the complexities and uncertainties of the modern global economy.

One company that has embarked on this agile journey is PepsiCo.

The food and beverage giant has been facing increasing pressure from changing consumer preferences, rising costs, and supply chain disruptions.

In response, PepsiCo has launched a company-wide agile transformation initiative called "Foresight."

Under this program, PepsiCo has reorganized its operations and supply chain teams into cross-functional "pods" that work closely together to identify and solve problems in real-time.

Each pod is focused on a specific product line or geographic region and is empowered to make quick decisions based on the latest data and insights.

For example, when the COVID-19 pandemic disrupted PepsiCo's supply chain in early 2020, the company's agile pods were able to quickly pivot their strategies and tactics.

One pod in the United States worked closely with local suppliers to secure alternative sources of key ingredients, while another pod in Europe rapidly adjusted production schedules to meet changing demand patterns.

By leveraging advanced analytics and digital tools, PepsiCo's agile pods were able to gain real-time visibility into their operations and supply chain, enabling them to anticipate and respond to disruptions more effectively. They also used virtual collaboration platforms to maintain close communication and alignment across different functions and regions.

Another company that has embraced agile operations and supply chain management is Zara, the Spanish fast-fashion retailer.

Zara is renowned for its ability to quickly design, produce, and deliver new clothing styles to stores around the world, often in a matter of weeks.

At the heart of Zara's agile approach is a close collaboration between its design, production, and distribution teams. Designers work closely with store managers to gather real-time feedback on customer preferences and trends, which they use to rapidly prototype and test new styles. Production teams are located close to Zara's stores, allowing them to quickly manufacture and deliver small batches of new products as needed.

Zara's agile supply chain is supported by advanced technology and data analytics. The company uses RFID tags to track inventory levels and customer behaviour in real-time, enabling it to optimize its production and distribution processes based on actual demand. Zara also leverages artificial intelligence and machine learning to predict future trends and optimize its design and pricing strategies.

By embracing agile principles, Zara has been able to achieve remarkable speed and flexibility in its operations and supply chain. The company can respond to changing customer needs and market conditions in a matter of days or weeks, rather than months or years. This has enabled Zara to maintain its competitive edge and grow its global presence, even in the face of increasing competition and economic uncertainty.

Of course, implementing agile operations and supply chain management is not without its challenges.

It requires a significant shift in mindset and culture, as well as investments in new technologies and capabilities. Companies need to be willing to break down traditional silos and hierarchies, empower teams to make decisions and take risks, and foster a culture of continuous learning and improvement.

They also need to be attuned to the unique challenges and opportunities of their specific industry and geographic context. For example, in regions with less developed infrastructure or more complex regulatory environments, agile approaches may need to be adapted to account for longer lead times, greater uncertainty, or different cultural norms.

Despite these challenges, the benefits of agile operations and supply chain management are clear.

By becoming more responsive, resilient, and customer-centric, companies can not only survive but thrive in today's rapidly changing business environment. As the examples of PepsiCo and Zara illustrate, those who embrace agility as a core principle of their operations and supply chain will be well-positioned to seize new opportunities and create lasting value for their customers and stakeholders.

Streamlining Operations with Agile Techniques

In today's business landscape, companies across industries are seeking ways to optimize their operations and stay ahead of the competition.

One increasingly popular approach is to leverage agile techniques to streamline processes, improve efficiency, and drive continuous improvement. By embracing agile principles such as flexibility, collaboration, and iterative development, organizations can become more responsive to changing market conditions and customer needs.

A compelling example of a company that has successfully streamlined its operations using agile techniques is Bosch, the German multinational engineering and technology firm.

Bosch has been undergoing a digital transformation in recent years, with a focus on applying agile methodologies to its manufacturing and supply chain operations.

One key initiative has been the implementation of "agile production lines" in Bosch's factories. These modular, reconfigurable production systems allow the company to quickly adapt to changing product requirements and customer demands. By using smart sensors, real-time data analytics, and collaborative robots, Bosch can optimize its production processes on the fly, reducing waste, improving quality, and increasing productivity.

Bosch has also been experimenting with "agile logistics" approaches, such as using autonomous vehicles and drones for material handling and delivery. By leveraging these technologies in combination with advanced planning and optimization algorithms, the company can create more flexible and efficient supply chain networks that can respond rapidly to disruptions or changes in demand.

Another notable example of a company that has successfully streamlined its operations using agile techniques is Unilever, the multinational consumer goods giant.

Unilever has been on a journey to transform its operations and supply chain to become more agile and resilient in recent years.

A key initiative has been the implementation of "agile manufacturing" principles in Unilever's factories. The company has been investing in advanced technologies such as 3D printing, robotics, and digital twins to create more flexible and modular production systems. These systems allow Unilever to quickly reconfigure its production lines to accommodate different product variants or packaging formats, reducing changeover times and increasing overall equipment effectiveness.

Unilever has also been experimenting with "agile sourcing" approaches, such as using real-time data analytics and machine learning to optimize its procurement and inventory management processes. By leveraging these technologies, the company can dynamically adjust its supply plans based on changing demand signals, reducing waste and improving service levels.

Of course, implementing agile techniques to streamline operations requires more than just adopting new tools and methodologies.

Companies need to foster a culture of collaboration, transparency, and trust, where teams are empowered to take ownership and make decisions based on data and customer insights. They also need to invest in the necessary skills, processes, and governance structures to support agile ways of working at scale.

Moreover, agile techniques may need to be tailored to the specific needs and constraints of different industries and geographies.

For example, in highly regulated sectors such as pharmaceuticals or aerospace, agile approaches may need to be balanced with robust quality and compliance controls. In emerging markets with less developed infrastructure and talent pools, companies may need to adapt their agile practices to local realities and constraints.

Despite these challenges, the benefits of streamlining operations with agile techniques are clear and compelling.

By becoming more nimble, responsive, and customer-centric, companies can reduce costs, improve quality, accelerate innovation, and create sustainable competitive advantage. As the examples of Unilever and Bosch illustrate, those who successfully embed agility into their operations will be well-positioned to thrive in an increasingly dynamic and unpredictable business environment.

Building Flexibility and Resilience in Supply Chains

In the face of increasing global uncertainty and disruption, building flexibility and resilience in supply chains has become a top priority for companies across sectors. From trade tensions and tariff disputes to natural disasters and pandemics, the past few years have highlighted the fragility of traditional, linear supply chain models and the need for more agile and adaptive approaches.

This imperative has only been heightened by the rapidly changing prices of shipping lines and the shifting geopolitical landscape. As transportation costs fluctuate and trade relationships evolve, companies need to be able to quickly adjust their sourcing, production, and distribution strategies to maintain competitiveness and continuity.

One company that has been proactively building flexibility and resilience into its supply chain is Intel, the global semiconductor manufacturer.

Intel has long recognized the importance of agility in its operations, given the highly dynamic and competitive nature of the technology industry.

To enhance its supply chain resilience, Intel has been investing in a multi-sourcing strategy that reduces its dependence on any single supplier or region. The company has established a network of qualified suppliers across different geographies, and has been actively diversifying its sourcing base to mitigate the risk of disruptions or price volatility.

Intel has also been leveraging advanced analytics and machine learning to create a more intelligent and responsive supply chain.

By using real-time data and predictive modelling, the company can better anticipate demand fluctuations, optimize inventory levels, and adjust production schedules accordingly. This allows Intel to reduce waste, improve efficiency, and respond more quickly to changing market conditions.

Another example of a company that has successfully built flexibility and resilience into its supply chain is Nestlé, the world's largest food and beverage company.

Nestlé has been on a journey to transform its supply chain into a more agile and sustainable network that can adapt to the challenges and opportunities of the 21st century.

One of the key initiatives in this transformation has been the implementation of a "responsive supply chain" model that emphasizes flexibility, collaboration, and innovation.

Under this model, Nestlé has been working closely with its suppliers and customers to create a more transparent and aligned value chain that can quickly respond to changing needs and preferences.

For example, Nestlé has been using digital platforms and tools to enable real-time information sharing and collaboration across its supply chain.

By creating a common data ecosystem and using advanced analytics and simulation, the company can better coordinate its planning, execution, and optimization activities, and can make more informed and agile decisions.

Nestlé has also been experimenting with new technologies and business models to create a more flexible and resilient supply chain. For instance, the company has been piloting the use of blockchain to improve the traceability and transparency of its sourcing and production processes. It has also been exploring the potential of 3D printing and other additive manufacturing techniques to enable more localized and customized production.

By combining these initiatives with a strong focus on sustainability and social responsibility, Nestlé has been able to create a more agile and purpose-driven supply chain that can better withstand the challenges of a rapidly changing world. The company has reduced its environmental footprint, improved its supplier relationships, and enhanced its ability to innovate and grow in new markets.

Of course, building flexibility and resilience in supply chains is not a one-size-fits-all proposition.

Companies need to carefully assess their specific industry dynamics, risk profiles, and strategic priorities, and develop tailored approaches that balance agility with efficiency and reliability.

They also need to invest in the necessary capabilities and partnerships to support agile ways of working, such as digital technologies, collaborative platforms, and ecosystem relationships.

Moreover, as the examples of Intel and Nestlé illustrate, building flexibility and resilience in supply chains is not just a defensive play, but also an opportunity to create new sources of value and differentiation. By becoming more agile, responsive, and purpose-driven, companies can not only mitigate risks and disruptions, but also unlock new growth opportunities and stakeholder trust.

In an era of increasing uncertainty and change, building flexibility and resilience in supply chains has become a strategic imperative for companies across sectors. Those that can successfully navigate this challenge will be well-positioned to thrive in the face of adversity and seize the opportunities of the future.

Chapter 7: Agile Finance and Budgeting

In today's business landscape, traditional financial planning and budgeting processes often struggle to keep up. The need for agility and adaptability in financial management has never been more pressing, as companies navigate a world of increasing uncertainty and volatility.

Imagine a global manufacturing company, with operations spanning multiple continents and currencies.

For years, the company had relied on a traditional, annual budgeting process, where each business unit would submit its financial projections and resource requirements for the upcoming year, based on historical data and assumptions about future market conditions.

However, as the company expanded into new markets and faced increasing competition, this approach began to show its limitations.

The annual budget quickly became outdated as market conditions changed, and the company found itself unable to respond quickly to new opportunities or threats. Moreover, the budgeting process itself was time-consuming and resource-intensive, diverting attention and energy from more strategic priorities.

Recognizing the need for change, the company embarked on a journey to transform its financial management practices and adopt a more agile approach.

One of the key initiatives was the implementation of a rolling forecast process, where financial projections were updated on a quarterly basis, based on the latest market intelligence and business performance data.

This approach allowed the company to be more responsive to changing conditions and to allocate resources more dynamically based on evolving priorities. It also fostered greater collaboration and alignment between finance and other business functions, as teams worked together to continuously refine their plans and assumptions.

Another important aspect of the company's agile finance transformation was the adoption of advanced analytics and scenario planning tools.

By leveraging machine learning and predictive modelling, the company was able to generate more accurate and timely insights into key business drivers and risk factors, and to simulate different scenarios and contingencies.

This capability proved particularly valuable in navigating the challenges of currency volatility and geopolitical uncertainty. As trade tensions escalated and exchange rates fluctuated, the company was able to use sophisticated hedging strategies and financial instruments to mitigate its exposure and protect its margins.

For example, when the company's primary manufacturing hub was hit by a sudden devaluation of the local currency, the finance team was able to quickly model the impact on the company's cost structure and pricing, and to implement a series of targeted hedges and cost-saving measures to offset the impact.

The company also experimented with using cryptocurrency and central bank digital currencies (CBDCs) as a way to facilitate cross-border transactions and reduce its reliance on traditional banking channels. While these initiatives showed promise in terms of speed and efficiency, they also introduced new risks and uncertainties, such as the lack of regulatory clarity and the potential for market volatility.

Despite these challenges, the company's agile finance transformation yielded significant benefits in terms of increased visibility, flexibility, and resilience.

By adopting a more dynamic and data-driven approach to financial management, the company was able to make better-informed decisions, respond more quickly to changing conditions, and deliver more value to its customers and stakeholders.

Of course, the journey to agile finance is not a one-time event, but rather an ongoing process of learning, experimentation, and adaptation. Companies need to continually assess and refine their strategies and tactics based on evolving business needs and market realities, and to invest in the necessary skills, processes, and technologies to support agile ways of working.

They also need to foster a culture of collaboration, transparency, and trust, where finance is seen not just as a back-office function, but as a strategic partner and enabler of business value. This requires a shift in mindset and behaviour, as well as a willingness to challenge traditional assumptions and embrace new ways of thinking and doing.

As the example of the global manufacturing company illustrates, agile finance and budgeting can be a powerful tool for navigating the challenges and opportunities of today's volatile and uncertain business environment. By becoming more adaptive, responsive, and resilient, companies can position themselves for success in the face of adversity and change, and create lasting value for their customers, employees, and shareholders.

Adopting Agile Financial Planning and Forecasting

Today traditional financial planning and forecasting processes often fall short of providing the agility and responsiveness needed to navigate uncertainty and change. Annual budgets and static forecasts can quickly become outdated, leaving companies ill-equipped to seize new opportunities or mitigate emerging risks.

Consider the case of a fast-growing technology startup, operating in a highly competitive and dynamic market.

The company had been using a traditional, bottom-up budgeting process, where each department would submit its own spending plans and projections for the upcoming year, based on historical data and assumptions about future growth.

However, as the company scaled and entered new markets, this approach became increasingly cumbersome and ineffective.

The budgeting process took months to complete, and the resulting plan was often misaligned with the company's rapidly evolving priorities and objectives. Moreover, the static nature of the budget made it difficult to adapt to changing market conditions or customer needs.

To address these challenges, the company decided to adopt an agile approach to financial planning and forecasting.

One of the key initiatives was the implementation of a continuous planning process, where budgets and forecasts were updated on a rolling basis, based on real-time data and insights from across the organization.

Under this new approach, each department would provide regular updates on its performance and expectations, using a common set of metrics and assumptions.

The finance team would then consolidate and analyse this information, using advanced analytics and modelling tools to generate dynamic, scenario-based forecasts that could be easily adjusted as conditions changed.

This agile planning process allowed the company to be more responsive and proactive in its decision-making, as it could quickly identify and address potential risks or opportunities.

It also fostered greater collaboration and alignment between different parts of the organization, as teams worked together to continuously refine and optimize their plans based on shared goals and objectives.

Another important aspect of the company's agile financial planning transformation was the adoption of a more flexible and decentralized budgeting model. Instead of allocating fixed budgets to each department based on historical spending patterns, the company moved to a more dynamic and iterative funding approach, where resources were allocated based on the expected value and impact of specific initiatives or projects.

This approach allowed the company to be more agile and adaptive in its resource allocation, as it could quickly shift funding to high-priority areas or emerging opportunities. It also encouraged a more entrepreneurial and innovative mindset across the organization, as teams were incentivized to experiment and take calculated risks in pursuit of growth and value creation.

Of course, implementing an agile financial planning and forecasting process had its challenges. The company had to invest in new tools and technologies to support real-time data collection and analysis, as well as in training and change management to help employees adapt to new ways of working.

There were also concerns about the potential loss of control and accountability, as budgeting and planning became more decentralized and fluid. To mitigate these risks, the company put in place robust governance and risk management frameworks, as well as clear policies and guidelines around financial planning and reporting.

Despite these challenges, the benefits of adopting an agile approach to financial planning and forecasting were significant.

The company was able to make faster and more informed decisions, respond more quickly to changing market conditions, and allocate resources more effectively to drive growth and innovation.

Moreover, the agile planning process helped to break down silos and foster a more collaborative and transparent culture across the organization. By involving a broader range of stakeholders in the planning process and sharing information and insights more openly, the company was able to build greater trust and alignment around its strategic priorities and objectives.

As the example of the technology startup illustrates, adopting agile financial planning and forecasting can be a powerful way to navigate the challenges and opportunities of today's fast-paced and uncertain business environment. By becoming more adaptive, responsive, and data-driven in their approach to financial management, companies can position themselves for success in the face of change and disruption, and create lasting value for their customers, employees, and investors.

Leveraging Agile Budgeting for Competitive Advantage

In a business landscape characterized by rapid change and intense competition, companies that can allocate their resources quickly and effectively in response to new challenges and opportunities often gain a significant advantage over their rivals.

Traditional budgeting processes, which are often rigid, time-consuming, and backward-looking, can act as a barrier to agility and innovation.

Consider the case of a mid-sized pharmaceutical company that was facing increasing pressure from generic drug manufacturers and rising R&D costs.

The company had historically allocated its budget on an annual basis, with each department receiving a fixed amount of funding based on the previous year's spending, adjusted for inflation and other factors.

However, as the competitive landscape shifted and new opportunities emerged, such as the development of personalized medicine and digital health solutions, the company found that its budgeting process was holding it back.

The R&D team, in particular, was struggling to secure the resources it needed to pursue promising new drug candidates and technologies, as it was constrained by the fixed budget allocated at the beginning of the year.

To address this challenge, the company decided to adopt an agile budgeting approach, which allowed for greater flexibility and responsiveness in resource allocation.

Under this new model, budgets were set on a quarterly basis, with a portion of the overall budget held back in a central "innovation fund" that could be allocated to high-priority initiatives and projects as they emerged.

Each quarter, teams from across the organization would pitch their ideas and business cases to a cross-functional steering committee, which would evaluate the proposals based on their alignment with the company's strategic priorities, expected return on investment, and risk profile. The committee would then allocate resources from the innovation fund to the most promising initiatives, while also adjusting the budgets of existing projects and departments based on their performance and changing needs.

This agile budgeting approach allowed the company to be much more responsive to changing market conditions and customer needs.

When a new competitor entered the market with a disruptive technology, the company was able to quickly pivot and allocate resources to its own competing project, rather than being locked into a fixed budget that didn't allow for such flexibility.

Similarly, when the COVID-19 pandemic hit and demand for certain drugs and treatments skyrocketed, the company was able to rapidly scale up production and distribution by reallocating resources from less critical areas. This agility allowed the company to capture market share and build brand loyalty during a time of crisis, while also supporting public health efforts.

Implementing an agile budgeting approach required a significant shift in mindset and culture for the pharmaceutical company.

Many employees were initially resistant to the idea of giving up their fixed budgets and having to compete for resources on a quarterly basis. There were also concerns about the potential for short-termism and a lack of long-term planning.

To address these concerns, the company invested heavily in training and communication, helping employees to understand the benefits of agile budgeting and how it could support the company's overall strategy and vision. The finance team also worked closely with each department to develop clear performance metrics and KPIs that would be used to evaluate the success of each initiative and project.

Over time, the agile budgeting approach began to yield significant benefits for the pharmaceutical company. The R&D team was able to pursue a wider range of innovative projects and bring new drugs to market faster, while also reducing costs and improving efficiency. The company was also able to respond more quickly to changing customer needs and market trends, and to build a more engaged and empowered workforce.

Perhaps most importantly, the agile budgeting approach helped the company to build a more sustainable and resilient business model. By allocating resources based on strategic priorities and performance, rather than historical precedent, the company was able to focus on the areas that mattered most for its long-term success, while also maintaining the flexibility to adapt to new challenges and opportunities as they emerged.

As the pharmaceutical company's story illustrates, leveraging agile budgeting for competitive advantage is a powerful way for organizations to thrive in today's fast-paced and unpredictable business environment. By adopting a more flexible, responsive, and performance-driven approach to resource allocation, companies can unlock new sources of innovation and growth, while also building the agility and resilience needed to navigate an ever-changing landscape.

Chapter 8: Agile Human Resources and Talent Management

In this era of rapid change and disruption, organizations are increasingly recognizing the importance of agility in their human resources (HR) and talent management strategies.

As companies navigate new challenges and opportunities, they require a workforce that is adaptable, resilient, and capable of continuous learning and growth.

However, traditional HR practices, which often prioritize stability, predictability, and hierarchy, can hinder agility and innovation. To truly embrace agility, organizations must fundamentally reimagine their approach to attracting, developing, and retaining talent, as well as managing performance and rewards.

The Agile Talent Mindset

Cultivating an agile talent mindset is essential for organizations seeking to thrive in today's fast-paced and unpredictable business environment. This mindset emphasizes adaptability, curiosity, and a willingness to learn and grow continuously.

One company that has successfully fostered an agile talent mindset is Netflix.

Netflix has built a culture that values freedom, responsibility, and innovation, and that attracts and retains employees who share these values. Its talent philosophy is based on the idea of a "dream team," which consists of high-performing individuals who are able to operate with a high degree of autonomy and accountability. To build this dream team, Netflix has developed a unique approach to talent acquisition and management, which emphasizes the following principles:

1. Hire the best: Netflix seeks out the most talented and experienced individuals in their respective fields, and is willing to pay top dollar to attract and retain them.

2. Encourage freedom and responsibility: Netflix gives its employees a high degree of freedom to make decisions and take risks, but also expects them to take full responsibility for the outcomes of their actions.

3. Promote transparency and feedback: Netflix encourages open and honest communication, and provides employees with regular feedback on their performance and development.

4. Reward performance, not tenure: Netflix's compensation system is based on individual performance and contributions, rather than tenure or job level.

By embracing these principles, Netflix has been able to build a highly engaged and productive workforce that is able to adapt and innovate in response to changing market conditions and customer needs.

Attracting and Retaining Agile Talent

Attracting and retaining agile talent requires a different approach than traditional recruiting and retention strategies.

Companies must look beyond conventional resumes and credentials and instead seek out candidates who demonstrate agile mindsets and behaviours, such as adaptability, collaboration, and continuous learning.

One organization that has successfully attracted and retained agile talent is the United States Air Force (USAF).

The USAF faces a unique challenge in attracting and retaining top talent in a highly competitive job market, particularly in fields such as cybersecurity, artificial intelligence, and space operations.

To address this challenge, the USAF has developed a new talent management framework called "Talent Marketplace," which is designed to match airmen with job opportunities based on their skills, experiences, and preferences, rather than just their rank or career field.

Under this framework, airmen create online profiles that highlight their skills, experiences, and career goals, and can browse and apply for job opportunities across the Air Force. Managers can also search for and recruit talent based on specific skills and requirements.

The Talent Marketplace also includes a range of development and learning opportunities, such as training programs, mentorship, and job rotations, which are designed to help airmen build new skills and experiences and advance their careers.

By creating a more agile and personalized approach to talent management, the USAF has been able to attract and retain a more diverse and skilled workforce, while also improving job satisfaction and retention rates.

Another example of an organization that has successfully attracted and retained agile talent is Patagonia, the outdoor clothing and gear company.

Patagonia has a strong culture of environmental sustainability and social responsibility, which attracts employees who share these values.

To retain these employees, Patagonia offers a range of unique benefits and perks, such as paid time off for volunteering, on-site childcare, and flexible work arrangements. The company also invests heavily in employee development and growth, offering a range of training and development programs, as well as opportunities for cross-functional collaboration and experimentation.

By creating a culture that aligns with its employees' values and provides opportunities for growth and development, Patagonia has been able to build a highly engaged and loyal workforce that is committed to the company's mission and values.

Designing Agile Performance Management Systems

Traditional performance management systems, which often rely on annual reviews and ratings, can be rigid, time-consuming, and demotivating for employees. To support agility and innovation, organizations need to design performance management systems that are more flexible, collaborative, and focused on continuous improvement.

One company that has successfully redesigned its performance management system to support agility is Regeneron Pharmaceuticals, a leading biotechnology company.

Regeneron recognized that its traditional performance management process, which relied on annual goal-setting and reviews, was not effective in driving innovation and collaboration. In response, Regeneron implemented a new performance management system called "R-Evolve," which emphasizes ongoing feedback, coaching, and development.

Under this system, managers and employees have regular check-ins throughout the year to discuss progress, challenges, and opportunities for growth.

These check-ins are guided by a set of "power skills," which are the key behaviours and competencies that Regeneron believes are essential for success, such as critical thinking, communication, and adaptability. Managers and employees use these power skills as a framework for setting goals, providing feedback, and identifying development opportunities.

Regeneron also implemented a new rewards and recognition system that is more closely tied to individual and team contributions, rather than just job level or tenure. This includes spot bonuses, peer recognition, and other forms of non-monetary recognition that celebrate employees' achievements and contributions.

By creating a more agile and collaborative performance management system, Regeneron has been able to foster a culture of innovation and continuous improvement, while also improving employee engagement and retention.

Another example of an organization that has successfully designed an agile performance management system is the United States Navy.

The Navy recognized that its traditional performance evaluation system, which relied on annual fitness reports and rankings, was not effective in developing leaders who could adapt to rapidly changing environments and make decisions under pressure.

In response, the Navy implemented a new performance management system called "Sailor 2025," which emphasizes ongoing feedback, coaching, and development, as well as a more holistic view of sailor performance and potential.

Under this system, sailors receive regular feedback and coaching from their supervisors, peers, and subordinates, using a set of leadership competencies that are aligned with the Navy's values and mission.

Sailors also have opportunities to participate in leadership development programs, such as mentoring, job rotations, and education and training.

The Navy also implemented a new talent management system that is designed to identify and develop high-potential sailors and match them with career opportunities that align with their skills and interests. This includes a new "talent marketplace" that allows sailors to browse and apply for job opportunities across the Navy, as well as a range of career development tools and resources.

By creating a more agile and responsive performance management system, the Navy has been able to improve sailor engagement, retention, and readiness, while also building a more diverse and skilled workforce that is able to adapt to new challenges and opportunities.

Building an agile workforce requires a fundamental shift in HR and talent management practices, from a focus on stability and predictability to a focus on adaptability, collaboration, and continuous learning. This shift requires organizations to rethink their approach to attracting, developing, and retaining talent, as well as managing performance and rewards. It also requires a new kind of leadership that is more supportive, empowering, and focused on creating an environment where employees can thrive and grow.

By embracing these changes, organizations can create a more engaged, innovative, and resilient workforce that is able to adapt to new challenges and opportunities in an increasingly complex and uncertain business environment.

As the examples of Netflix, the USAF, Patagonia, Regeneron, and the Navy illustrate, building an agile workforce is not only possible but also essential for success in today's rapidly changing world.

Activity: Agile Talent Management Puzzle

Instructions:

Below, you will find a series of clues related to the concepts and examples discussed in Chapter 8 on agile talent management.

Each clue will lead you to a specific word or phrase. Once you have discovered all the words or phrases, use them to fill in the blanks in the final statement at the bottom of the puzzle. Some clues may require you to research online or refer back to the chapter for more information.

Enjoy the puzzle!

Clues:

1. The company that famously abolished its annual performance review process in 2012 and implemented a new system called "Check-in."

2. The term used to describe the ongoing feedback and coaching conversations between managers and employees at Adobe.

3. The global consulting firm that implemented a new performance management system called "Performance Snapshot."

4. The four key dimensions used in Deloitte's "Performance Snapshot" framework: business results, leadership, ______, and development.

5. The online marketplace for short-term rentals that has a strong focus on culture and values, emphasizing diversity, belonging, and innovation.

6. The unique hiring process used by Spotify that focuses on assessing candidates' potential for _______ and adaptability.

7. The term used to describe the small, cross-functional groups that work together at Spotify to deliver specific features and improvements.

8. The global music streaming service known for its agile and innovative culture, which emphasizes autonomy, trust, and collaboration among its employees.

Final Statement:

Embracing _(1)_'s "_(2)_" system, _(3)_'s "Performance Snapshot" framework focusing on business results, leadership, _(4)_, and development, _(5)_'s emphasis on culture and values, _(6)_'s unique hiring process assessing _(7)_ and adaptability, and _(8)_'s agile and innovative culture are all examples of how organizations can successfully attract, retain, and manage agile talent in today's fast-paced business environment.

————xx————

By completing the puzzle, readers will reinforce their understanding of agile talent management practices and how they contribute to organizational success in today's dynamic business landscape.

Part 3: Agile Transformation and Scaling

Chapter 9: Leading an Agile Transformation

———

Today organizations must embrace agility to remain competitive and responsive to changing market demands.

However, transforming an organization to become truly agile is no easy feat. It requires a fundamental shift in mindset, culture, and processes, as well as strong leadership to guide the transformation journey.

This chapter will explore the key aspects of leading an agile transformation, including assessing organizational readiness for agility and developing a roadmap for change.

We will also examine real-world examples of organizations that have successfully navigated the challenges of agile transformation to emerge as more adaptable, innovative, and resilient.

Embracing the Agile Mindset

Before embarking on an agile transformation, it is essential to understand what it means to be truly agile. At its core, agility is about the ability to quickly and effectively respond to change, whether it be shifting customer preferences, new market opportunities, or disruptive technologies.

However, achieving agility is not simply a matter of implementing new processes or tools. Rather, it requires a fundamental shift in mindset and culture, one that values collaboration, experimentation, and continuous learning over rigid hierarchies and top-down decision-making.

One company that has successfully embraced the agile mindset is Bosch, the German multinational engineering and technology company. Bosch recognized that in order to stay ahead of the curve in an increasingly digital world, it needed to become more agile and innovative.

To achieve this, Bosch launched a company-wide agile transformation program called "Smart Work@Bosch," which aimed to foster a culture of collaboration, experimentation, and continuous improvement.

The program included a range of initiatives, such as:

1. Agile training and coaching for employees at all levels of the organization

2. The creation of cross-functional teams focused on solving specific customer problems

3. The introduction of new tools and methodologies, such as design thinking and lean startup

4. The establishment of innovation labs and accelerators to incubate new ideas and business models

By embracing the agile mindset and empowering its employees to think and act more entrepreneurially, Bosch has been able to accelerate its digital transformation and remain at the forefront of innovation in its industry.

Assessing Organizational Readiness for Agility

Before launching an agile transformation, it is important to assess the organization's readiness for change.

This involves evaluating the current state of the organization across a range of dimensions, including:

1. Culture: Is the organization's culture conducive to agility, or are there deeply entrenched behaviours and attitudes that may resist change?

2. Structure: Is the organization structured in a way that enables cross-functional collaboration and rapid decision-making, or are there silos and bureaucratic barriers that impede agility?

3. Processes: Are the organization's processes designed to support agility, or are they rigid and inflexible?

4. Technology: Does the organization have the technology infrastructure and tools in place to enable agile ways of working, or are there legacy systems that hinder collaboration and innovation?

5. Leadership: Are the organization's leaders committed to the agile transformation and willing to model the behaviours and mindset required for success?

One tool that can be used to assess organizational readiness for agility is the Agile Maturity Model (AMM). Developed by Deloitte, the AMM provides a framework for evaluating an organization's current state of agility across five levels of maturity:

1. Initial: The organization is aware of agile but has not yet begun to implement agile practices.

2. Managed: The organization has started to experiment with agile practices in specific areas but has not yet scaled agile across the enterprise.

3. Defined: The organization has established a set of standardized agile practices and processes that are consistently applied across the enterprise.

4. Measured: The organization has established metrics and key performance indicators (KPIs) to track the effectiveness of its agile practices and continuously improve.

5. Optimized: The organization has fully embraced agility as a way of working and has a culture of continuous improvement and innovation.

By using the AMM to assess its current state of agility, an organization can identify areas of strength and weakness and develop a targeted plan for improvement.

Developing a Roadmap for Agile Transformation

Once an organization has assessed its readiness for agility, the next step is to develop a roadmap for the agile transformation.

This roadmap should be tailored to the unique needs and goals of the organization, but there are some common elements that should be included:

1. Vision and objectives: What is the organization trying to achieve through the agile transformation, and how will success be measured?

2. Leadership and governance: Who will lead the transformation effort, and what governance structures will be put in place to ensure alignment and accountability?

3. Piloting and scaling: Where will the organization start with agile practices, and how will it scale those practices across the enterprise over time?

4. Capability building: What skills and capabilities will need to be developed to support the agile transformation, and how will the organization build those capabilities?

5. Change management and communication: How will the organization manage the change process and communicate the benefits and progress of the transformation to stakeholders?

One company that has successfully developed and executed an agile transformation roadmap is LEGO Group, the Danish toy manufacturer.

LEGO faced significant challenges in the early 2000s, including declining sales and increased competition from digital entertainment. To turn things around, LEGO embarked on an agile transformation journey that involved rethinking its entire operating model. The company started by piloting agile practices in its product development and marketing functions, and then gradually scaled those practices across the enterprise.

LEGO also invested heavily in building the capabilities of its employees, providing training and coaching on agile methodologies and mindsets. The company established a network of agile coaches and champions to support the transformation effort and ensure that agile practices were being consistently applied.

Perhaps most importantly, LEGO's leadership team was fully committed to the agile transformation and modelled the behaviours and mindset required for success. They communicated a clear vision for the future of the company and empowered employees to take ownership of the transformation effort.

As a result of its agile transformation, LEGO was able to significantly improve its financial performance and regain its position as a leading innovator in the toy industry. The company's revenue grew from $1.6 billion in 2006 to $5.9 billion in 2019, and it has consistently ranked among the most innovative companies in the world.

Overcoming Challenges and Resistance to Change

Of course, leading an agile transformation is not without its challenges. One of the biggest obstacles is often resistance to change from employees who are comfortable with the status quo and fearful of the unknown.

To overcome this resistance, leaders must communicate a compelling vision for the future and help employees understand how the agile transformation will benefit them personally and professionally. They must also create a safe and supportive environment for experimentation and learning, where employees feel empowered to take risks and try new things.

Another common challenge is the tendency for organizations to focus too narrowly on specific agile practices or tools, rather than the underlying mindset and principles. Leaders must ensure that the agile transformation is not just a superficial change, but a fundamental shift in the way the organization thinks and operates.

One company that has successfully navigated these challenges is ING, the Dutch multinational banking and financial services corporation.

ING recognized that in order to remain competitive in an increasingly digital world, it needed to become more agile and customer-centric.

To achieve this, ING launched an agile transformation program called "One Agile Way of Working," which aimed to break down silos and create a more collaborative and responsive organization. The program involved a range of initiatives, such as:

1. The creation of cross-functional "squads" focused on specific customer journeys and value streams

2. The introduction of new agile roles, such as product owners and agile coaches

3. The establishment of a "Minimum Viable Product" (MVP) approach to product development, which emphasized rapid experimentation and iteration

4. The adoption of new tools and technologies, such as cloud computing and DevOps, to enable faster and more efficient delivery

However, ING also recognized that the success of the agile transformation depended on more than just new processes and tools.

The company invested heavily in culture change, providing training and coaching to help employees develop an agile mindset and embrace new ways of working.

ING's leadership team also played a critical role in the transformation, communicating a clear vision for the future and modeling the behaviors and mindset required for success. They empowered employees to take ownership of the transformation effort and provided the resources and support needed to make it a reality.

As a result of its agile transformation, ING has been able to significantly improve its customer satisfaction and employee engagement scores, while also reducing costs and increasing speed to market. The company has become a recognized leader in agile banking and has inspired other organizations around the world to embark on their own agile transformation journeys.

Leading an agile transformation is a complex and challenging undertaking, but it is also an essential one for organizations that want to remain competitive and responsive in today's rapidly changing business environment.

Chapter 10: Measuring the Impact of Agility

As organizations embrace agility and undergo transformations to become more adaptable and responsive, it is crucial to measure the impact of these efforts.

By establishing key agility metrics and key performance indicators (KPIs), organizations can assess the effectiveness of their agile practices, identify areas for improvement, and make data-driven decisions to optimize their processes and outcomes.

This chapter will explore the importance of measuring the impact of agility, discuss essential agility metrics and KPIs, and provide real-world examples of organizations that have successfully leveraged data and feedback to continuously improve their agile practices.

The Importance of Measuring Agility

Measuring the impact of agility is essential for several reasons:

1. Justifying investment:

Agile transformations require significant time, effort, and resources. By measuring the impact of agility, organizations can demonstrate the value of their investment to stakeholders and justify continued support for agile initiatives.

2. Identifying areas for improvement:

Agility metrics and KPIs can help organizations pinpoint areas where their agile practices are falling short, enabling them to focus their improvement efforts where they will have the greatest impact.

3. Facilitating continuous improvement:

By regularly measuring and analysing agility metrics, organizations can establish a feedback loop that enables them to continuously refine and optimize their agile practices over time.

4. Benchmarking performance:

Agility metrics can help organizations compare their performance against industry benchmarks and best practices, providing valuable insights into their relative strengths and weaknesses.

Key Agility Metrics and KPIs

There are numerous metrics and KPIs that organizations can use to measure the impact of agility, depending on their specific goals and context.

However, some common agility metrics include:

1. Cycle time:

Cycle time measures the amount of time it takes for a work item (e.g., a user story or feature) to move from the backlog to completion. By reducing cycle time, organizations can deliver value to customers more quickly and respond to changing needs more efficiently.

2. Lead time:

Lead time measures the amount of time from when a customer request is received until it is delivered. Like cycle time, reducing lead time can help organizations deliver value more quickly and improve customer satisfaction.

3. Throughput:

Throughput measures the number of work items completed over a given period (e.g., per week or per sprint). Increasing throughput can help organizations deliver more value to customers and improve their overall productivity.

4. Defect density:

Defect density measures the number of defects per unit of work (e.g., per story point or per line of code). By reducing defect density, organizations can improve the quality of their products and services and reduce the amount of time and effort required for rework.

5. Customer satisfaction:

Customer satisfaction measures how well an organization is meeting the needs and expectations of its customers. By regularly collecting and analysing customer feedback, organizations can identify areas for improvement and ensure that they are delivering value that meets customer needs.

Example: Salesforce's Agility Metrics

Salesforce, the global leader in customer relationship management (CRM) software, has successfully leveraged agility metrics to drive continuous improvement and optimize its development processes.

One of the key metrics that Salesforce tracks is cycle time.

By measuring the amount of time it takes for a work item to move from the backlog to completion, Salesforce can identify bottlenecks and inefficiencies in its development process and take steps to address them.

For example, Salesforce noticed that certain types of work items, such as those related to compliance or security, tended to have longer cycle times than others.

By digging deeper into the data, Salesforce was able to identify the root causes of these delays, such as a lack of standardized processes or insufficient communication between teams.

To address these issues, Salesforce implemented a number of changes, such as:

1. Establishing clear policies and procedures for handling compliance and security-related work items

2. Improving communication and collaboration between development teams and other stakeholders, such as legal and security teams

3. Automating certain compliance and security checks to reduce manual effort and accelerate the development process

As a result of these changes, Salesforce was able to significantly reduce cycle times for compliance and security-related work items, from an average of 60 days to just 14 days.

This not only improved the efficiency of Salesforce's development process but also helped the company deliver value to customers more quickly and respond to changing needs more effectively.

Continuously Improving Based on Data and Feedback

Measuring the impact of agility is not a one-time event, but rather an ongoing process of continuous improvement.

By regularly collecting and analysing data and feedback, organizations can identify opportunities for improvement and take steps to optimize their agile practices over time.

One approach to continuous improvement is the use of retrospectives. Retrospectives are regular meetings where agile teams reflect on their recent work, identify what went well and what could be improved, and develop action plans for future sprints.

By conducting retrospectives on a regular basis (e.g., after each sprint), teams can continuously refine their processes and practices based on real-world experience and feedback. This not only helps teams become more efficient and effective over time but also fosters a culture of continuous learning and improvement.

Example: Spotify's "Fail Wall"

Spotify, has embraced a culture of continuous improvement and learning from failure.

One way that Spotify encourages this culture is through the use of a "fail wall."

The fail wall is a physical or virtual space where Spotify employees can share their failures and the lessons they learned from them. By publicly acknowledging and discussing failures, Spotify aims to normalize the idea that failure is a natural part of the innovation process and that it is okay to take risks and make mistakes as long as we learn from them.

The fail wall has become an important part of Spotify's culture of continuous improvement.

By regularly sharing and discussing failures, Spotify employees are able to identify common pitfalls and develop strategies for avoiding them in the future. This not only helps Spotify become more resilient and adaptable as an organization but also fosters a culture of psychological safety where employees feel comfortable taking risks and pushing boundaries.

Example: Etsy's Continuous Improvement Kata

Etsy, the global online marketplace for handmade and vintage goods, has successfully leveraged a continuous improvement framework called the "Improvement Kata" to drive ongoing optimization of its agile practices.

The Improvement Kata is a structured approach to continuous improvement that involves four key steps:

1. Understand the direction: Clearly define the goals and objectives of the improvement effort.

2. Grasp the current condition: Analyze the current state of the process or system being improved, using data and metrics to identify areas for improvement.

3. Establish the next target condition: Define the desired future state of the process or system, including specific, measurable targets for improvement.

4. Iterate toward the target condition: Develop and execute a series of small, incremental experiments to move toward the target condition, using data and feedback to continuously refine and optimize the approach.

Etsy has applied the Improvement Kata to a wide range of agile practices, from its product development process to its customer support operations.

By using a structured, data-driven approach to continuous improvement, Etsy has been able to achieve significant gains in efficiency, quality, and customer satisfaction.

For example, Etsy used the Improvement Kata to optimize its product development process, with the goal of reducing cycle time and improving throughput. By analysing data on its current process and conducting a series of small experiments, Etsy was able to identify and eliminate bottlenecks, streamline communication and collaboration between teams, and automate certain tasks to reduce manual effort.

As a result of these improvements, Etsy was able to reduce its average cycle time by 50%, from 28 days to just 14 days.

This not only helped Etsy deliver value to customers more quickly but also freed up capacity for teams to take on additional work and innovate more rapidly.

Measuring the impact of agility is essential for organizations that want to optimize their agile practices and achieve sustained success in today's fast-paced, ever-changing business environment. By establishing key agility metrics and KPIs, organizations can assess the effectiveness of their agile practices, identify areas for improvement, and make data-driven decisions to drive continuous optimization.

However, measuring the impact of agility is not a one-time event, but rather an ongoing process of continuous improvement. By regularly collecting and analyzing data and feedback, conducting retrospectives, and applying structured improvement frameworks like the Improvement Kata, organizations can continuously refine and optimize their agile practices over time, becoming more efficient, effective, and resilient in the face of change.

Ultimately, the organizations that will thrive in the age of agility are those that embrace a culture of continuous learning and improvement, using data and feedback to drive ongoing optimization and innovation. By measuring the impact of agility and continuously improving based on those insights, organizations can unlock the full potential of their agile transformations and achieve sustained success in the years to come.

121

Part 4: Agility in Action
Chapter 11: Case Studies of Agile Organizations

Throughout this book, we have explored the principles, practices, and benefits of agility, and how organizations can embark on their own agile transformations.

However, to truly understand the impact of agility, it is valuable to examine real-world examples of companies that have successfully embraced agile ways of working and are thriving as a result.

In this chapter, we will dive into case studies of organizations from a variety of industries that have undergone agile transformations and are reaping the benefits of increased flexibility, adaptability, and innovation.

We will explore the unique challenges and opportunities they faced, the strategies and approaches they employed, and the lessons learned and best practices that have emerged from their experiences.

Case Study : Siemens - Agility in Industrial Manufacturing

Siemens, the global industrial manufacturing giant, has been on a journey of agile transformation in recent years, seeking to become more responsive to changing customer needs and market conditions.

With over 380,000 employees worldwide and a diverse portfolio of products and services, Siemens faced significant challenges in breaking down silos, increasing transparency and collaboration, and fostering a culture of innovation.

To address these challenges, Siemens launched a company-wide agile transformation program called "Siemens Agile." The program aimed to:

1. Establish cross-functional teams focused on delivering end-to-end value to customers

2. Empower teams with greater autonomy and decision-making authority

3. Foster a culture of experimentation, learning, and continuous improvement

4. Leverage technology to enable seamless collaboration and transparency across the organization

One of the key initiatives under the Siemens Agile program was the creation of "Agile Innovation Labs."

These labs brought together cross-functional teams of experts from different business units and geographies to work on strategic innovation projects, using agile methodologies such as Scrum and Design Thinking.

The Agile Innovation Labs have been a resounding success, delivering a range of breakthrough innovations in areas such as renewable energy, smart infrastructure, and digital healthcare.

For example, one lab developed a new AI-powered system for predictive maintenance of industrial equipment, which has helped Siemens' customers reduce downtime and improve operational efficiency.

Another critical aspect of Siemens' agile transformation has been the emphasis on continuous learning and skill development. Siemens has invested heavily in training and coaching programs to help employees develop the skills and mindset needed to thrive in an agile environment, such as collaboration, adaptability, and customer-centricity.

As a result of these efforts, Siemens has seen significant improvements in key metrics such as time-to-market, customer satisfaction, and employee engagement. The company has also been recognized as a leader in agile innovation, with several of its projects winning industry awards and accolades.

Case Study : USAA - Agility in Financial Services

USAA, the financial services company that serves members of the U.S. military and their families, has long been known for its customer-centric approach and commitment to innovation.

However, like many organizations in the financial services industry, USAA faced challenges in keeping pace with the rapid changes in technology, customer expectations, and regulatory requirements.

To address these challenges, USAA embarked on an agile transformation journey focused on three key areas:

1. Developing agile leaders who could inspire and empower teams to work in new ways

2. Creating a culture of experimentation and learning, where teams were encouraged to take risks and learn from failures

3. Adopting agile methodologies and tools across the organization, from software development to business operations

One of the most impactful initiatives under USAA's agile transformation was the creation of "Member Experience Teams."

These cross-functional teams were responsible for designing and delivering end-to-end experiences for USAA's members, from researching customer needs to developing and launching new products and services.

The Member Experience Teams used agile methodologies such as Kanban and Lean Startup to rapidly prototype and test new ideas, gather feedback from customers, and iterate based on that feedback. This approach enabled USAA to deliver a range of innovative solutions, such as mobile banking apps, virtual assistants, and personalized financial advice, that have helped the company maintain its position as a leader in customer satisfaction and loyalty.

Another key aspect of USAA's agile transformation has been the emphasis on continuous improvement and learning.

The company has established a range of feedback mechanisms, such as regular retrospectives and customer surveys, to gather insights and identify areas for improvement. USAA also invests heavily in employee training and development, with a particular focus on agile skills such as design thinking, user experience design, and data analytics.

As a result of these efforts, USAA has achieved significant improvements in key metrics such as time-to-market, customer satisfaction, and employee engagement. The company has also been recognized as a leader in agile innovation, with several of its initiatives winning industry awards and accolades.

Case Study : Zappos - Agility in E-commerce

Zappos, the online shoe and clothing retailer, has long been known for its unique culture and customer-centric approach.

However, as the company grew and expanded into new product categories and markets, it faced challenges in maintaining its culture and agility in the face of increasing complexity and scale.

To address these challenges, Zappos embarked on a radical agile transformation that involved completely restructuring the organization around self-managing teams. Under this new structure, known as "Holacracy," teams are organized around specific roles and responsibilities, rather than traditional job titles and hierarchies.

Each team is responsible for setting its own goals, making decisions, and delivering value to customers, with minimal oversight from management. This approach has enabled Zappos to become more agile and responsive to changing customer needs and market conditions, while also empowering employees to take ownership of their work and continuously improve their processes.

One of the key benefits of Zappos' agile transformation has been the ability to rapidly experiment and innovate. Teams are encouraged to try new ideas and approaches, and to learn from failures as well as successes. This has enabled Zappos to launch a range of innovative products and services, such as its "Zappos Adaptive" line of clothing and shoes for people with disabilities, and its "Zappos for Good" program, which donates shoes and clothing to people in need.

Another critical aspect of Zappos' agile transformation has been the emphasis on culture and values.

The company has a strong set of core values, such as "Deliver WOW Through Service" and "Embrace and Drive Change," that guide everything it does. Zappos invests heavily in employee training and development to ensure that everyone in the organization understands and embodies these values, and regularly assesses its culture through employee surveys and feedback mechanisms.

As a result of these efforts, Zappos has achieved significant improvements in key metrics such as customer satisfaction, employee engagement, and innovation. The company has also been recognized as a leader in agile and customer-centric business practices, with its unique culture and approach studied and emulated by organizations around the world.

Lessons Learned and Best Practices

While each of the organizations profiled in these case studies faced unique challenges and opportunities in their agile transformations, there are several common lessons learned and best practices that have emerged:

1. Start with a clear vision and purpose:

Successful agile transformations are guided by a clear vision and purpose that everyone in the organization understands and is committed to achieving.

2. Empower teams and individuals:

Agile organizations empower teams and individuals to make decisions, take ownership of their work, and continuously improve their processes, with minimal oversight from management.

3. Foster a culture of experimentation and learning:

Agile organizations encourage experimentation, risk-taking, and learning from failures as well as successes, recognizing that innovation often requires iteration and adaptation.

4. Invest in skills and capabilities:

Successful agile transformations require significant investments in training, coaching, and development to ensure that employees have the skills and capabilities needed to thrive in an agile environment.

5. Leverage technology and data:

Agile organizations leverage technology and data to enable seamless collaboration, transparency, and decision-making, and to continuously measure and improve their performance.

6. Focus on delivering value to customers:

Ultimately, the success of an agile transformation is measured by the value it delivers to customers, whether through faster time-to-market, higher quality products and services, or more personalized and responsive experiences.

The case studies and best practices explored in this chapter demonstrate the transformative power of agility in today's fast-paced and ever-changing business environment.

By embracing agile principles and practices, organizations across industries and geographies have been able to achieve significant improvements in key metrics such as innovation, customer satisfaction, and employee engagement, while also becoming more resilient and adaptable in the face of disruption and change.

However, as these case studies also illustrate, agile transformations are not easy or straightforward. They require significant investments in time, resources, and leadership commitment, as well as a willingness to challenge long-held assumptions and ways of working.

Ultimately, the organizations that will thrive in the age of agility are those that are willing to embrace change, empower their people, and continuously learn and adapt.

Chapter 12: Agility and the Future of Work

As we have seen throughout this book, agility has become an essential capability for organizations seeking to thrive in an increasingly complex and rapidly changing business environment.

However, the impact of agility extends far beyond the realm of organizational strategy and performance. In many ways, agility is also shaping the future of work itself, from the way we collaborate and communicate to the skills and capabilities that will be most valuable in the years to come.

In this final chapter, we will explore the intersection of agility and the future of work, with a particular focus on how agility enables remote and hybrid work arrangements and what organizations can do to prepare for the workforce of the future.

We will also examine some of the key trends and challenges that are likely to shape the future of work, and how agility can help organizations navigate these shifts and seize new opportunities for growth and innovation.

The Rise of Remote and Hybrid Work

One of the most significant ways in which agility is shaping the future of work is through the rise of remote and hybrid work arrangements.

With the rapid advancement of digital technologies and the increasing globalization of business, more and more organizations are embracing the idea of a distributed workforce, where employees can work from anywhere in the world and collaborate seamlessly across time zones and geographies.

The COVID-19 pandemic has only accelerated this trend, forcing many organizations to quickly adapt to remote work arrangements and rethink traditional notions of office-based work. While the transition to remote work has not been without its challenges, it has also revealed the many benefits of a more flexible and agile approach to work, from increased productivity and employee satisfaction to reduced costs and environmental impact.

Case Study: GitLab - The All-Remote Company

One organization that has fully embraced the potential of remote work is GitLab, a software development company that has been operating as an all-remote company since its founding in 2014.

With over 1,300 employees spread across more than 65 countries, GitLab has built a thriving and highly productive remote work culture that leverages agile principles and practices to enable seamless collaboration and communication. At the heart of GitLab's remote work model is a set of core values and practices that prioritize transparency, accountability, and continuous improvement.

For example, all meetings at GitLab are conducted via video conferencing and are recorded and transcribed for anyone in the company to access. This radical transparency helps to build trust and alignment across the organization, while also enabling asynchronous communication and collaboration.

GitLab also places a strong emphasis on documentation and knowledge sharing, with a comprehensive handbook that captures all aspects of the company's operations and culture.

This handbook serves as a central resource for employees, enabling them to quickly find answers to common questions and navigate the complexities of remote work.

To support its remote work model, GitLab has invested heavily in digital tools and platforms that enable seamless collaboration and communication, such as Slack, Zoom, and its own product, GitLab. The company also provides a range of resources and support for employees to help them thrive in a remote work environment, from home office stipends to mental health and wellness programs.

As a result of these efforts, GitLab has been able to build a highly engaged and productive remote workforce, with employee satisfaction and retention rates that far exceed industry averages. The company has also been recognized as a leader in remote work and has inspired many other organizations to embrace more flexible and agile work arrangements.

Preparing for the Workforce of the Future

While remote and hybrid work are certainly important aspects of the future of work, they are far from the only trends that organizations need to be prepared for.

In the coming years, a range of other factors, from the increasing automation of work to the growing demand for new skills and capabilities, are likely to reshape the workforce in significant ways.

To thrive in this new landscape, organizations will need to embrace agility not just in their work practices, but also in their approach to talent management and workforce development. This will require a fundamental shift in mindset, from viewing employees as static resources to be managed and optimized, to seeing them as dynamic and evolving assets to be nurtured and developed over time.

Case Study: AT&T - Reskilling for the Future

One organization that has taken a proactive approach to preparing for the workforce of the future is AT&T, the global telecommunications giant.

Recognizing the rapid pace of technological change and the growing demand for new skills and capabilities, AT&T launched a massive reskilling initiative in 2013 aimed at transforming its workforce for the digital age.

The initiative, known as "Future Ready," provides a range of learning and development opportunities for employees, from online courses and bootcamps to on-the-job training and mentorship programs.

The goal is to help employees develop the skills and capabilities they need to thrive in a rapidly changing industry, whether that means learning new programming languages, mastering data analytics, or developing soft skills like collaboration and communication.

To support this initiative, AT&T has invested heavily in its learning and development infrastructure, creating a range of digital platforms and tools that enable employees to access training and resources from anywhere in the world. The company has also partnered with leading universities and training providers to develop custom curricula and programs tailored to its specific needs and goals.

One of the key aspects of AT&T's Future Ready initiative is its emphasis on continuous learning and development.

Rather than viewing reskilling as a one-time event, the company encourages employees to engage in ongoing learning and development throughout their careers, with regular check-ins and assessments to track progress and identify areas for improvement.

As a result of these efforts, AT&T has been able to build a more agile and adaptable workforce, with employees who are better equipped to navigate the challenges and opportunities of the digital age.

The company has also seen significant improvements in employee engagement and retention, as well as increased innovation and productivity across the organization.

The Importance of Soft Skills

While technical skills and capabilities will certainly be important in the workforce of the future, they are far from the only factors that will determine success.

In fact, many experts predict that so-called "soft skills," such as emotional intelligence, creativity, and adaptability, will become increasingly valuable in the years to come.

This is because the most complex and challenging problems of the future will require not just technical expertise, but also the ability to collaborate effectively, think critically, and adapt to changing circumstances. In a world where machines and algorithms are increasingly able to perform routine tasks and calculations, it will be the uniquely human skills and capabilities that will be most valuable.

Case Study: Airbnb - Cultivating a Culture of Belonging

One organization that has recognized the importance of soft skills and has made them a core part of its culture and values is Airbnb, the global hospitality platform. From its earliest days, Airbnb has placed a strong emphasis on creating a culture of belonging, where employees feel valued, supported, and empowered to bring their whole selves to work.

To cultivate this culture, Airbnb has invested heavily in employee development and well-being, with a range of programs and initiatives designed to support the physical, mental, and emotional health of its workforce. For example, the company offers generous parental leave policies, unlimited vacation time, and a range of wellness benefits, from gym memberships to mindfulness training.

Airbnb also places a strong emphasis on diversity, equity, and inclusion, with a range of initiatives designed to create a more diverse and representative workforce and to foster a culture of belonging for all employees. This includes employee resource groups, diversity and inclusion training, and a commitment to pay equity and fair hiring practices.

To support the development of soft skills and capabilities, Airbnb has created a range of learning and development programs that focus on areas like emotional intelligence, communication, and leadership. The company also encourages employees to pursue their passions and interests outside of work, recognizing that these experiences can help to build resilience, creativity, and adaptability.

As a result of these efforts, Airbnb has been able to build a highly engaged and motivated workforce, with employees who are passionate about the company's mission and values and who are equipped with the skills and capabilities needed to thrive in a rapidly changing industry. The company has also been recognized as a leader in employee experience and has inspired many other organizations to prioritize culture and belonging as key drivers of business success.

The Path Forward

As we have seen throughout this chapter, the future of work is likely to be shaped by a range of trends and challenges, from the rise of remote and hybrid work to the growing demand for new skills and capabilities.

To thrive in this new landscape, organizations will need to embrace agility not just in their work practices, but also in their approach to talent management and workforce development.

This will require a willingness to experiment with new models and approaches, to invest in the learning and development of employees, and to create a culture that values diversity, inclusion, and belonging. It will also require a recognition that the skills and capabilities that are most valuable today may not be the same ones that are needed tomorrow, and that ongoing learning and adaptation will be essential for success.

Ultimately, the organizations that are able to navigate these challenges and seize the opportunities of the future of work will be those that are able to harness the power of agility to create more dynamic, resilient, and innovative workforces. By embracing agility as a core value and a key driver of business success, these organizations will be well-positioned to thrive in.

Acknowledgements

As I come to the end of this book, I want to take a moment to express my deepest gratitude to everyone who has been a part of this journey with me. Writing "Agility Unbound" has been a labor of love, and I could not have done it without the support, encouragement, and engagement of my readers and the wider community.

First and foremost, I want to thank you, my readers, for taking the time to explore the world of agility with me. Your curiosity, enthusiasm, and willingness to learn have been a constant source of inspiration for me, and I have been truly humbled by the positive feedback and stories you have shared with me along the way.

I also want to thank my partners and collaborators, thank you for your support and guidance throughout this process. Your insights and perspectives have helped to shape the direction and content of this book, and I am grateful for the opportunities I have had to learn from and work with you.

I also want to acknowledge the wider agility community, both online and offline, for the valuable contributions you have made to the field. From the thought leaders and practitioners who have shared their knowledge and experience, to the organizations and individuals who have embraced agility as a way of working and living, your stories and examples have been a constant source of inspiration for me.

Finally, I want to thank my family and loved ones, who have been my rock throughout this journey. Your love, patience, and understanding have been invaluable, and I could not have done this without you.

As I look to the future, I am excited about the possibilities that lie ahead. I believe that agility has the power to transform not just organizations, but also individuals and communities, and I am committed to continuing to explore and share the latest insights and best practices in this field.

I hope that "Agility Unbound" has been a valuable resource for you, and that it has inspired you to embrace agility in your own life and work. Whether you are a business leader, a team member, or simply someone who is curious about the future of work, I believe that agility has something to offer everyone.

Thank you again for joining me on this journey, and I look forward to continuing the conversation with you in the years to come.

With gratitude,

Asish Dash

Also by ASISH DASH

The Shy Entrepreneur
Insights From A Shy Entrepreneur
Insights from a Shy Entrepreneur : Turning Slowdown into
Opportunity

Standalone
Entrepreneurship and Dharma : Gita Inspired Insights
The LLM Advantage: How to Unlock the Power of Language
Models for Business Success
Agility Unbound : Harnessing the Power of Adaptive
Organizations

Watch for more at https://in.linkedin.com/in/dashasish.

About the Author

Asish Dash, is the Founder of Grazing Minds - the fastest growing sustainable consulting edtech platform.

Asish defines himself as 3E. (Engineer, Economist and Entrepreneur) an alumnus of world's Top 10 university and various other institutes.

Frugality in business, is his passion and so is creating low cost self sustaining business models.He loves talking, studying and decoding business models and innovation around it.

After 3 successful startups, He is all into sharing information. He believes writing books is one way in which he can connect to my audiences apart from the consulting he does on LinkedIn.

Though some of his opinions may be termed as brash and opinionated - but he says, he is not here to appease any corporations or lobbies!!

Read more at https://in.linkedin.com/in/dashasish.

About the Publisher

Grazing Minds publishing is the subsidiary of Grazing Minds Research and Consulting, the knowledge arm founded by serial entrepreneur Asish Dash. It provides consulting and edtech services in the field of management, finance, banking, logistics and hospitality.